Also from the Boys Town Press

Books

The Well-Managed Classroom
Teaching Social Skills to Youth
Effective Skills for Child-Care Workers
The Ongoing Journey: Awakening Spiritual Life in At-Risk Youth
Working with Aggressive Youth
Caring for Youth in Shelters
Helping Teens Unmask Sexual Con Games
The Boys Town Family Preservation Program
The SAY Books: Group Therapy for Sexually Abused Youth
I Think of My Homelessness
Letters from the Front
Boys Town: A Photographic History

Videos

Helping Your Child Succeed
Teaching Responsible Behavior
Videos for Parents Series
Sign With Me: A Family Sign Language Curriculum
Read With Me: Sharing the Joy of Storytelling with Your Deaf Toddler

For a free Boys Town Press catalog, call 1-800-282-6657.

Common Sense Parenting

A Practical Approach from Boys Town

By

Raymond V. Burke
Ronald W. Herron

© 1992, Father Flanagan's Boys' Home, Boys Town, NE 68010
ISBN 0-938510 - 33 - 9

Dear Parent,

Love, patience and understanding. These are wonderful qualities for parents to possess. However, these qualities are sometimes not enough for you to be an effective parent and raise well-behaved children.

What is missing? The answer is in your hands. It's a book that supplies practical methods for teaching children. It's Common Sense Parenting.

The methods we present were developed at Boys Town. They are logical and easy to learn and use. They have proven successful and effective with thousands of boys and girls who have come to us seeking help and guidance. We know these methods can help your family too.

Whether you are a parent who wishes to "brush up" on your parenting skills, or an excited "rookie" with your first child, or an exasperated parent with rebellious or difficult children, this book can help you.

Sometimes, all parents need is a little help and encouragement. Other times, they need to completely change what they're doing and try a new method. Common Sense Parenting will help you understand your child's behavior and give you a framework for correcting your child, encouraging positive behavior, and even fostering change within yourself. Parenting is the most exciting challenge of your life. Make the most of it.

We applaud you for taking the time to read and use our Common Sense Parenting book. We thank you for all of the wonderful work you are doing right now with your kids. We encourage you to use our book to become an even better parent. Meet the challenges of parenthood with confidence. Bring to the task all of the love and energy you can muster. Stir in the skills learned in Common Sense Parenting and you've got a powerful mixture. It's well worth the effort.

Sincerely,

Father Val J. Peter, JCD, STD
Executive Director

Acknowledgments

This book would not have been possible without the generous work of many helping hands along the way. A huge thanks goes to all of the Boys Town staff, past and present, who have contributed to the development of the ideas we share on the following pages. Too numerous to mention individually, their personal contributions have laid the foundation for Common Sense Parenting.

A special thanks goes to all of the parents who have participated in the program over the years; to the Common Sense Parenting staff for their creative ideas and tireless work; to the Boys Town Press for their detailed editing and suggestions; to the Print Shop for late nights and early mornings in an effort to help us meet deadlines; to Dr. Patrick Friman for the "Time Out" appendix; and to all of the Family Based Programs staff, especially Karen Authier, Director, for encouragement in times of need.

Table of Contents

Introduction

Common Sense Parenting

A miracle happened the day you became a parent. Do you remember the joy you felt when your child was born? A newborn baby is one of life's greatest gifts. That little life was in your hands. From that day forward, you assumed all of the joy and pain that comes with being a parent.

As children grow, there are times when the joy of parenthood is severely tested. The simplicity of taking care of a baby changes to the complexity of dealing with a holy terror, a pudgy whirlwind who always manages to find trouble around every corner. Next come calls from elementary school teachers, fights with other kids, messy rooms, and an emerging earthy vocabulary. Then the teen years! Cars, dates, parties, testing adult limits, wild music, far-out clothing, and theories about how to change the world are the next strangers to fill your dance card.

With all of that to frustrate and worry you, is it any wonder that you may occasionally doubt your effectiveness as a parent? No one said it was going to be easy. But then again, no one said it was ever going to be this tough, either.

Parenting *isn't* easy, we know that. We, at Boys Town, have been parents to more than 17,000 young people. That's a big family. And, it adds up to a lot of wonderful experience in parenting, and a lot of wonderful experiences in raising kids. In order to share what we have learned with concerned people like you, we have developed and refined a practical method to help parents become more effective in parenting. This method is used not only on the campus here at Boys Town, but also in many homes just like yours, by parents we have helped in our *Common Sense Parenting Program.*

Parents mean well and try to do what's best for their kids, using all of the resources they can muster. For many parents, this means times of painful trial and error, times of sadness or self-doubt.

All parents occasionally need some help and advice when they are having a tough time with their kids. That's why we wrote this book.

We want to help you rediscover the joy of parenthood by enhancing your parenting skills. We want to show you how to discipline your child through teaching. And we want to give you a blueprint for parenting that has proved to be effective for thousands of families.

We know that your children are precious. As parents, you want what is best for them. That requires patience, compassion, love, and understanding. We don't have all the answers. But we believe our ideas about parenting will benefit both you and your children, and in so doing, bring you closer together.

How to Use This Book

Parents are some of the busiest people we know. They usually are juggling several schedules, have a list of things to do that is a mile long, and have little or no time for "extras" such as reading this book. With that in mind, we've set up this book in short chapters that should take no more than a few minutes to read. Of course, you can sit down and read for hours if you like, but that amount of time probably is just too hard for you to find.

This book is to be read and also used as a workbook. Writing down how you would respond to your children's behavior is the first step toward learning a more effective way to parent. Because writing is so important, please take the time to complete the exercises we have provided.

Each chapter outlines a parenting skill and gives examples for using that skill in a variety of situations. There also are exercises that help you put the skill into practice with your child. We suggest reading each chapter and doing all of the exercises provided. Then, pick up the book again when you are experiencing some of the rough spots and need a reminder of how to handle a problem.

This book does not present a specific theory of child care. There are plenty of those books on the market already. What we do offer are methods of interacting with your children—practical ways to help you help your kids. We hope that you use these methods so often that they become second-nature to you. Both you and your children will benefit. As you use these skills, you should expect behavior changes in your children.

Just one note about the change process. Change takes time. It took your kids years to learn the behaviors they now display. Learning new behaviors won't occur overnight. Things often get worse before they get better. It's like remodeling a house. You live with a lot of dust and dirt before you ever have things the way you want them. And, it takes a heap of work and perseverance to complete the house. The same holds true with remodeling your kids' behavior.

Expect some pitfalls. Understand that it takes time and effort. And, look at each improvement as a step in the right direction. You are well aware of the frustrating moments that parents experience. There are no magical cures for all these problems, but the skills in this book have helped thousands of parents deal with and prevent the situations that cause the most difficulty for families.

We hope that you, like so many other parents, find these skills to be practical, useful, and beneficial.

The Foundation

Chapter 1

Punishment vs. Teaching

Discipline is commonly misunderstood. As parents, we may each take a different approach to discipline. This may include punishment, correction, and/or guidance. Before we discuss our approach to discipline, please take a moment to answer the following questions about the way you deal with your children and their problems. Indicate your answers with a checkmark.

Exercise 1

		YES	NO
1.	Do you find yourself arguing with your kids?	☐	☐
2.	Do you feel like you're always correcting your kids?	☐	☐
3.	Do you often get your child to promise that he or she won't do something again?	☐	☐
4.	Do you fight with your child a lot?	☐	☐
5.	Do you sometimes respond with a big punishment for a relatively minor misbehavior?	☐	☐
6.	Do you sometimes threaten action that you know you won't carry out?	☐	☐
7.	Do you find yourself saying things to your child that you later regret saying?	☐	☐
8.	Do you repeat instructions time and time again?	☐	☐
9.	Do you often give in to your child's demands?	☐	☐
10.	Do you find that the more you punish, the more your child misbehaves?	☐	☐

If you answered "Yes" to most of these questions, you're definitely using punishment with your kids. If you answered "Yes" to two or more of these questions, you're still using some methods of punishment. You're not alone. Most parents, as a recent survey on parenting indicated, use punitive or unpleasant responses when their kids misbehave. This means parents yell, scold, call their kids names, or use physical punishment. The use of punishment is commonplace. And, we won't try to convince you that punishment doesn't work. It does. But, that doesn't mean parents should use it; punishment is not the best way to discipline children.

We understand that there are certain situations where some parents feel punishment can be effective and useful, if for no other reason than they feel something has to be done immediately. For example, when your 3-year-old runs into the street, grabbing him quickly out of the street and giving him a swift swat on the bottom can show him how dangerous that situation is. If a swat was used for each misbehavior, however, it would lose its effectiveness.

Also, our research has shown that as children get older, punishment loses effectiveness. Swatting a 16-year-old usually results in some type of retaliation and long-term problems for both parent and child.

Inappropriate Punishment

For our purposes, we define inappropriate punishment as something that is harsh and unreasonable, violent and harmful. Corporal punishment such as hitting, slapping, or punching hurts children, emotionally as well as physically.

Inappropriate punishments also include such behaviors as screaming, belittling, ridiculing, and isolating. The key ingredient to all inappropriate punishments is the harm they cause to a child's development. Corporal punishment, especially, makes parents feel pretty bad, too. Parents don't like the fact that they lost their cool.

Then why do parents use inappropriate punishment so often?

First of all, because it seems to get an immediate change in behavior. Sometimes, it gives us short-term results that seem effective. The first few times we yelled at the kids, they got quiet. Yelling has to work, right? Wrong. In the short run, inappropriate punishment can get what we want, but over time, it results in all sorts of problems for us and our children.

A second reason parents use inappropriate punishment is that they are not sure of what else to do in those situations. They are angry and frustrated and react to what their child said or did—almost like it was automatic. Hitting, yelling, and spanking are common punishments when parents react without thinking.

The third reason probably has been felt by all parents at one time or another—the fear of losing their authority. Parents have a fear that if they aren't tough enough, their kids will run roughshod over them, and the kids will be in control, not the parents. As parents feel the need to become tougher, to let the kids really know "they mean business," it leads them to use inappropriate punishment.

The last reason parents use inappropriate punishment is because no one taught them any other way. They learned by the models set for them; they learned from their parents. There's nothing wrong with this, we all learned from our parents. But, if a person's parents used inappropriate punishment, it is likely that they will use the same types of punishment (or do just the opposite and be overly permissive).

Please go to page 7 now and complete Exercise 2.

In your responses in Exercise 2, did you list any inappropriate punishments? Did you yell, threaten, or maybe even use physical punishment with your child? If you did, how did you feel afterwards? How do you think your child felt?

If you used inappropriate punishment, there's a good chance that your kids responded by yelling back, getting angry, or mumbling under their breath and walking away. In any case, they probably didn't feel very good about the situation—and neither did you. There's also a real good chance they didn't learn what they should do to avoid trouble in the future. Inappropriate punishment does not teach a child what to do; it only tells a child what not to do.

Exercise 2

Take a few minutes and jot down some of the times you remember misbehaving as a child and how your parents responded to you.

Misbehavior	**Parents' Response**
1. _____	1. _____
2. _____	2. _____
3. _____	3. _____
4. _____	4. _____

Now write down some of the things your own children do that you dislike. Then write down how you respond to their misbehavior.

Misbehavior	**Parents' Response**
1. _____	1. _____
2. _____	2. _____
3. _____	3. _____
4. _____	4. _____

Here are some other negative side effects of inappropriate punishment:

- It hurts children's self-esteem; children don't feel good about themselves after being hit or slapped, or yelled at, or made fun of.

- Punishment often results in revenge. Children want to get back at the person who punished them.

- Punishment damages relationships between parents and their children; children may want to avoid their parents altogether.

- Punishment can have a snowball effect. If one punishment doesn't work, parents often try a harsher one; a parent's response can escalate from requests to commands, to yelling, to hitting.

Appropriate Teaching

The focus of this entire book is to show you how to teach your children in a better way, without having to resort to the use of punishment. In *Common Sense Parenting*, we use what we call "**Appropriate Teaching**." All of the skills outlined in this book provide the foundation for appropriate teaching to take place.

Appropriate Teaching provides a positive and effective approach to problem behavior. Appropriate teaching is:

- **Specific** — you let your children know exactly what they did wrong.

- **Consistent** — you help your children understand the relationship between what they did and what happened as a result of their actions.

- **Concrete** — you give your children clear examples of how to improve in the future.

- **Positive** — you help your children learn self-discipline (to be in control of their actions and expressions of emotion).

- **Interactive** — you give your children a chance to show what they have learned. You are an active part of the learning process. You and your children work together toward a common goal.

- **Informative** — you become the teacher, the coach, as you give information that helps your children learn to solve problems.

In other words, Appropriate Teaching helps build self-esteem, teaches kids to get along well with others, and gives them the skills to make their own decisions.

Appropriate Teaching uses guidance rather than control. Children are much more likely to learn when they are treated with affection and pleasantness than when they are treated with anger and physical punishment. It provides a positive framework for necessary learning to take place.

Appropriate Teaching tells kids what they did wrong and how to correct it. If you are pleasant, firm, consistent, and able to give clear messages, you will be teaching effectively.

Common Sense Parenting consists of all of the qualities we have mentioned in Appropriate Teaching. These teaching methods work best when combined with the love and concern you have for your child.

Notes

Exercise 3

In the following examples, decide whether the parent used appropriate teaching or inappropriate punishment, and circle your answer.

1. Mike is playing with the TV video game. Johnny doesn't want to wait his turn, so he walks up and unplugs the game. Mike hits him with a Ping-Pong paddle. Mom hears what's going on, comes in, lifts Mike up, shakes him, and says, "Don't hit your brother!"

   Appropriate Teaching or

   Inappropriate Punishment

2. Sally and her friend are walking into the living room and talking about the new girl in school. Sally's mom overhears her tell her friend that they shouldn't play with the new girl anymore because she doesn't wear neat clothes. Mom asks the girls to sit down and they talk about how clothes shouldn't determine how someone feels about another person. Mom says it is what's inside a person that is important, not what's on the outside.

   Appropriate Teaching or

   Inappropriate Punishment

3. Dad tells Ty that he can't go outside to shoot baskets because Ty has homework to finish. Ty gets angry, stomps his feet, and complains how unfair his father is. Dad tells Ty that they need to talk about Ty's behavior. First, Ty needs to calm down and stop yelling. Moments later, after Ty has settled down, Dad explains to Ty that he needs to learn how to accept "No" for an answer.

   Appropriate Teaching or

   Inappropriate Punishment

4. Felicia draws a picture on the living room wall with a red crayon. She finds Mom, shows her the picture, and asks her if she likes it. Mom spanks Felicia and sends her to her room. She also tells Felicia that she doesn't draw very well.

   Appropriate Teaching or

   Inappropriate Punishment

In this exercise, appropriate teaching was used in examples 2 & 3. Was it easy to recognize the difference between appropriate teaching and inappropriate punishment?

Exercise 4

Describe what you would do if your child behaved like each child in the following examples.

1. Mike, your 15-year-old son, is 30 minutes late coming home from his friend's house. When you tell him you've been worried and feel it's important for him to be home on time, he yells, "I'll stay out as long as I damn well please!" and stomps down the hall to his room.

   *What would you do?*_____

   _____

   _____

   _____

   _____

2. Bridget, your 11-year-old daughter, received a detention in school for throwing a pencil at a fellow student and arguing with her teacher.

   *What would you do?*_____

   _____

   _____

   _____

   _____

3. Pat is active for a 6-year-old boy and frequently climbs on furniture, despite being told not to. You're on the phone when you hear him jumping off the coffee table and onto the couch. Suddenly, you hear a crash in the living room.

   *What would you do?*_____

   _____

   _____

   _____

   _____

4. Bobbie, age 4, knows how to get her way—especially at dinner. She throws her food and screams whenever anyone tries to talk with someone other than her. She just threw her mashed potatoes into the middle of the table, spilling some of the dinner drinks.

   What would you do? _____

   _____

   _____

   _____

   _____

There are many possible answers to the scenarios in Exercise 4. As we explain more about Appropriate Teaching, it will be interesting for you to come back and read the answers you gave here.

In the next chapters, we'll look at ways to improve parenting by:

1) being clear and specific when we teach, and

2) understanding the relationships between behaviors and their consequences.

Chapter 2

Clear Messages

"You've got a lousy attitude!"

"Shape up, Judy. Stop being so naughty."

"You were a good boy at the store."

These are common statements made by parents. But, do children really understand what the parents mean? We must remember that children are concrete thinkers; they don't grasp the full meaning of words that are abstract or vague. A "lousy attitude" does not give a child enough information to know what needs to be changed. A clear message might be, "You walked away from me when I asked you to do something, and mumbled 'Get off my back.'" This gives the child specific information. One of our goals as parents is to *give our kids messages they understand.*

Giving clear messages is one key to appropriate teaching. Parents need to specifically tell their children what needs to be done and how to do it. They need to tell their children when they've done well. They also need to correct their children when they've messed up and help them learn from their mistakes. Finally, parents need to teach their children how to think for themselves and solve problems.

But before this can happen, parents must know how to communicate clearly with their children. They must be specific, focus on what their children are doing or saying, and describe their children's behaviors.

Everyone has a general idea of what behaviors are, but to make sure we're on the same wavelength, let's take a look at a clear definition that can help parents give clear messages.

Behaviors

Behavior is what people do or say – anything a person does that can be seen, heard, or measured.

Here's a descriptive list of behaviors:

1. My daughter talks on the phone for one hour at a time.

2. When I ask my son to do something, he rolls his eyes and walks away.

3. When my kids come home from school, they put their books away and ask if there's anything that needs to be done around the house.

4. When I tell my daughter her jeans are too tight, she whines and screams, "Why are you such a bitch?"

5. My son helped me put away the dishes, then he rinsed the sink and swept the kitchen floor.

It is easy to understand what we mean by actions that can be seen or heard. You see your son slap his brother. You hear your daughter singing to her baby sister. But what do we mean by measuring a behavior? Think of it this way: You can count how long a person lays on a couch by the length of time that elapses. Laying on the couch is a behavior; it's something that person does. But you can't count how long a person has been lazy. Laziness is a perception.

Exercise 1

List four of your child's typical behaviors. Remember to focus on what is said and done.

1. _____

2. _____

3. _____

4. _____

Terms like "hyperactive," "naughty," "irresponsible," etc., are far from clear, concrete descriptions. These words describe perceptions; people see or hear something and form mental impressions of another person. As that person's behaviors are observed, perceptions are formed. The problem is that when these perceptions are conveyed to others they are easily misunderstood and can mean different things to different people. For children, this can be confusing; for teens, this can lead to arguments. "Irresponsible" to one parent may mean not coming home on time or leaving the kitchen a mess. To another parent, irresponsible may mean not helping around the house or not putting the lawn mower away. When parents teach their children, they need to describe behaviors, not perceptions, in order to give clear messages.

For you to give clear messages, you must first watch what your child does or says. Then, clearly and specifically tell your child what they did or did not do. Use words that you know your child will understand. For younger children, use short sentences and easily understood words. As they get older, adjust your language to fit their age and level of comprehension.

Have you ever listened to a sporting event on the radio? If you have, you know that a good sports announcer can make you visualize what is happening through his descriptions. You can see every play in your mind. He is giving a verbal replay of the action taking place. As parents, we need to be just as clear to our kids.

In order to give clear messages, it will help to describe the following:

- **Who** — Who is involved, who is being praised, whose behavior is being corrected.

- **What** — What just happened, what was done well, what needs to be improved or changed.

- **When** — When the behavior happened, when you want something.

- **Where** — Where the behavior occurred.

How you give messages also is very important. Here are several points that will help you convey clear messages to your children:

1. **Have your child look at you**. It's more likely that he or she will hear what you say and follow through on any requests. Our experience has taught us that eye contact is a key to giving and receiving clear messages.

2. **Look at your child**. This shows that you are paying attention and allows you to see your child's reaction to what you say. Give your child your full attention.

3. **Use a voice tone that fits the situation**; firm when giving correction, friendly when giving compliments, etc.

4. **Be aware of your facial expexpressions and body language**. For example, you might smile when you are happy about something your child has done, or frown when you are displeased.

5. **Eliminate as many distractions as possible**. Try to find a quiet area when you can talk to your child.

6. **Try to position yourself so that you are at eye level with your child**. Avoid intimidating your child by standing over him or her.

One final thought about clear messages: The most important part of being specific whenscribing your children's misbehavior is that they understand that you dislike their *behavior*, not *them*. You are upset and displeased with *the way your child is acting*. You still love your child; that's why you are taking the time to teach another way to behave.

Exercise 2

Circle the statements that give clear messages.

1. "Billy, why can't you act your age when company comes?"

2. "When we get to the store, please be a nice girl."

3. "Jim, would you please rake the back-yard, put the leaves in a big plastic bag, and put the bag on the front curb?"

4. "That was a nice story you wrote for English class, Sam."

5. "Sally, you need to stop talking right now."

6. "Reggie, don't eat like a pig."

7. "Veronica, when you chew your food, you should keep your mouth closed."

8. "Chuck, after school you are to come right home. Don't stop to play. Call me at work as soon as you get home."

9. "Billy, thank you for sitting still and not talking in church."

Statements 3, 5, 7, 8, and 9 are examples of clear messages. The other statements were not clear. They didn't describe specific behaviors.

Let's change these vague statements so that the person gets a clear message:

1. "Billy, you're whining about your sister taking your toy. I'd like you to go in the family room and pleasantly ask her to give it back."

2. "When we get to the store, remember that we aren't buying any candy. OK? I'd like you to help me pick out the things on our list and put them in the cart. You can also push the shopping cart. OK?"

4. "Sam, you did a nice job on that story for English class. You used complete sentences and all of the grammar was correct. The topic of prejudice was excellent! It was really controversial and interesting."

6. "Reggie, you're eating with your fingers and making grunting noises while you eat. I'd like you to eat with a fork, take small bites, and not make any noises."

These statements include descriptions of what each child said or did. It's more likely that the child will receive a clear message.

Framework for Giving Clear Messages

If you noticed, most of the previous nine statements followed a general pattern. We have a reason for that. We've found that giving parents a framework really helps them give clear messages. The first two parts of that framework (when correcting a behavior) are as follows:

1. **Describe what happened**. Tell your child what needs to be changed or stopped. Say something like "What you're doing now is..." or "You did..." , "You said...", etc.

2. **Describe what you want done.** Your child needs to know what you expect of him or her. Say something like "What I'd like you to do is..." or "Please go and ...", etc.

Notes _____

_____

_____

_____

_____

_____

_____

_____

_____

_____

_____

_____

_____

_____

Examples

1. *Describe what happened*—"Johnny, you left the milk out on the counter, and there are potato chip crumbs on the floor."

   Describe what you want done — "Please go out to the kitchen and put the milk in the refrigerator. Then sweep the floor and throw the crumbs away in the trash."

2. *Describe what happened* — "Mrs. Johnson called and said that on your way home, you rode your bike through her flowers."

   Describe what you want done — "I'd like you to go back over to her house and apologize to her. Then ask her if you can do anything to make up for going through her flowers."

3. *Describe what happened* — "Sandy, your music is too loud."

   Describe what you want done — "Please turn it down and shut your door."

4. *Describe what happened*—"What you're doing now is arguing with me."

   Describe what you want done — "I'd appreciate it if you would be quiet and let me finish talking. Then you can have your turn to speak. OK?"

A similar framework can be used when you are pleased with your child's behavior:

1. *Show your approval*. Say something like, "You really did a nice job with...," or "Thanks for..." or "That's fantastic! You..."

2. *Describe what was done well.* "...sweeping and mopping the floor," or "...playing quietly with your sister," or "...studied hard all week and got a 'B' on your test."

This can be done in one sentence. For example, "Thanks for taking the shovel back to Mr. Jones." This may sound very basic, but it is extremely important that your child hears your approval and knows exactly what was done right. Remember to give clear, positive messages!

Examples

1. *Show your approval* — "You really did a great job!"

   Describe what was done well — "It took a lot of time and effort to collect the money for the homeless."

2. *Show your approval*— "Thanks for helping out."

   Describe what was done well — "You took the time to help me make a grocery list and cut out the coupons. I really appreciate it."

3. *Show your approval* — "Awesome catch!"

   Describe what is being done well—"You stayed right in front of the ball and kept your eye on it. It was really hit hard!"

4. *Show your approval* — "Wow! You're downstairs already!"

   Tell what is being done well — "You set the alarm clock last night and got up on your own. That's three days in a row!"

Read the situations that follow. In place of the vague comments, write specific comments that give clear messages. We've done the first two as examples.

Situation: Your two children are arguing about who had the toy first.

Vague: "Cut that out!"

Specific: "What you're doing now is arguing about who had the toy first. What I'd like you to do is give me the toy and both of you sit quietly."

Situation: Your 3-year-old is using his spoon to eat his food.

Vague: "You're being such a good boy."

Specific: "All right! I'm so happy. You're using your spoon to eat! You're keeping all of the food on the spoon. Good job!"

Exercise 3

1. Situation: Your teenager throws her coat and books on the kitchen table.

   Vague: "What do you think you're doing?"

   Specific: (Describe what happened.)

   _____

   _____

   (Describe what you want done.) _____

   _____

   _____

   _____

2. Situation: Your 17-year-old spends 45 minutes on his homework instead of talking on the phone.

   Vague: "Gee, what got into you?"

   Specific: (Show your approval.)

   _____

   _____

   (Describe what was done well.) _____

   _____

   _____

3. Situation: Your 13-year-old argues with you about taking out the trash.

   Vague: "Don't you talk to me that way!"

   Specific: (Describe what happened.)

   _____

   _____

   (Describe what you want done.) _____

   _____

   _____

4. Situation: Your 9-year-old picked up his toys and put them away. He also picked up his clothes and put them in the laundry basket. Now, he wants to go out and play.

   Vague: "Thanks for being so neat. Sure, you can go out and play."

   Specific: (Show your approval.)

   _____

   _____

   (Describe what was done well.) _____

   _____

   _____

   _____

Continued on Page 16

5. Situation: Your 15-year-old son comes home one hour late.

   Vague: "Can't you tell time? You'll never go out again!"

   Specific: (Describe what happened.)

   _____

   _____

   (Describe what you want done.) _____

   _____

   _____

6. Situation: Your 14-year-old comes home with the highest grade she's ever received on a Math test.

   Vague: "Oh, that's nice."

   Specific: (Show your approval.) _____

   _____

   (Describe what was done well.) _____

   _____

   _____

7. Situation: Your 7-year-old leaves his bike in the driveway.

   Vague: "You are so irresponsible with your things."

   Specific: (Describe what happened.)

   _____

   _____

(Describe what you want done.) _____

_____

_____

8. Situation: Your 6-year-old asks for some candy. You tell her she will have to wait until after lunch and she says, "OK, Mommy."

   Vague: "That's a good girl."

   Specific: (Show your approval.) _____

   _____

   _____

   (Describe what was done well.) _____

   _____

   _____

9. Situation: Your 12-year-old is late getting up and refuses to get out of bed.

   Vague: "You're going to be late if you lay there all day."

   Specific: (Tell what happened.) _____

   _____

   _____

   (Describe what you want done.) _____

   _____

   _____

Now, try this at home with your children. Watch what they do and say for the next day or two. When you correct or compliment them, use the framework you just practiced. If you describe what your kids do or say, you'll give clearer messages.

Congratulations. Giving clear messages is the first step toward effective parenting. In the next chapters, we'll add another valuable technique—giving consequences.

You will find that as we move through the book, these techniques are used in many different situations. These techniques give loving parents a practical way to help their kids. Welcome to *Common Sense Parenting*.

Notes _____
_____
_____
_____
_____
_____
_____
_____
_____
_____
_____
_____
_____
_____

Chapter 3

Consequences

Consequences are at work all of the time. We run into them everyday—on our job, at home, with friends, and so on. If we don't get our work done, the boss criticizes us. If we don't remember to take the dog outside, he leaves a calling card on the carpet. If we compliment a friend, he returns the pleasantry. Consequences affect all of us, positively and negatively.

As parents, it helps to understand why giving consequences to our kids is so essential. Consequences teach kids to think. Consequences help children learn that their actions lead to results, both positive and negative. They learn that life is full of choices and the choices they make greatly influence what happens to them. Children, whose parents give appropriate consequences, learn successful ways to behave.

Consequences Change Behavior

As parents, knowing how to use consequences to teach our kids is so important. If consequences have the power to change behavior, it makes sense that we should use them to benefit our kids. You've probably used consequences frequently. "Grounding" your child, letting your teen go out on a weekend night, using "Time-Out," offering dessert only after the vegetables are finished, are all examples of consequences.

But, simply giving a consequence doesn't mean that kids are automatically going to change their behavior. Throughout this book, we emphasize that you learn to use a combination of clear messages and consequences when teaching your children. This combination, coupled with your love and affection, leads to effective parenting.

Let's look at some of the basic elements of effective consequences. There are two basic kinds of consequences — positive and negative.

- Positive consequences are things people like and are willing to work to get. Behavior that is followed by a positive consequence is more likely to occur again. Rewards are a form of positive consequences.

- Negative consequences are things people don't like and want to avoid. Basically, negative consequences encourage people to change their actions so that they won't receive more negative consequences. Behavior that is followed by a negative consequence is less likely to occur again (or will not occur as frequently). Removing a reward is a negative consequence.

Regardless of whether you feel these consequences have worked or not, let's take a look at qualities to consider when choosing an effective consequence:

Importance. The consequence has to mean something to your child. One way to find out what is important to your child is to watch what he does when he has free time. For example, if he likes to watch TV, invite friends over to your house, and ride his bicycle, then these are activities that are important to your child. These everyday and special activities can be used as

Exercise 1

Take some time to identify the consequences you now use with your children. List them in the following spaces.

List 3 negative consequences you give to your child:

1. _____

2. _____

3. _____

List 3 positive consequences you give to your child:

1. _____

2. _____

3. _____

consequences. Taking away or giving something that isn't of interest will probably have little effect on the behavior.

Immediacy. This means that parents should give a consequence right after a behavior occurs. If you can't give the consequence right away, give it as soon as possible. Delaying a consequence reduces its impact and weakens the connection between the behavior and the consequence. If you were to take away play time for something your 5-year-old did last week, she would not only be confused, but would also think that you were tremendously unfair.

Frequency. This refers to the number of times a consequence is given. If you give the same consequence too often or too seldom, it loses its effectiveness. Changes in the child's behavior will help parents determine whether

they are using a consequence too often or too seldom. For example, if you were to give your son a fruitcake (assuming he loved fruitcake) each time he helped around the house, he would soon want to avoid helping. He would get tired of fruitcake.

Degree. This means the severity or size of the consequence. Typically, parents should try to give the smallest consequence they think will be effective. This works for both positive and negative consequences. If you think that allowing your child to have a friend stay over Saturday night will be incentive enough for her to keep her room clean during the week, use that as the positive consequence. On the other hand, grounding your daughter for a month for not cleaning her room would be too big a negative consequence. A less severe consequence (not allowing her to have her friend stay over) would probably get the job done. Giving too much of a positive consequence may result in a "spoiled" child—one who gets too much for doing too little. On the other hand, giving too much of a negative consequence may result in a child who always feels punished.

Contingency. This is commonly called "Grandma's rule," because grandmothers used this long before it ever showed up in a book. Basically, it means that one activity (a privilege your child likes) is available after your child finishes an activity that you want done. For example:

> "You can watch TV after you have finished your homework."

> "You can go outside after you make your bed and put your dirty clothes in the laundry basket."

> "When you're finished with the dishes, you can call your friend."

These are all examples of Grandma's rule—giving a privilege after, not before, a specified task is completed. This contingency rule can be used with kids of all ages. As a quick practice, fill in the following blanks to see how it can work with your child.

"You can _____

_____ (something your

child likes) after you _____

_____" (some-

thing you want your child to do). Or,

"When you're finished with _____

_____, you can

_____."

When Consequences Don't Work

Occasionally, parents tell us that no matter what they try, consequences won't work with their kid. There could be several reasons for this. We'll just touch on a couple here.

Parents sometimes give many negative consequences and neglect giving positive consequences. As a result, the negative consequences lose their effectiveness. The parents aren't providing a balance between positive and negative consequences. The kids, logically, go elsewhere to get positive consequences. It's just too darn unpleasant being around their parents.

The second reason is that parents don't always give consequences enough time to work. They often expect a consequence to change a behavior the first time it is used. This isn't the case. Change takes time. Your kids didn't learn to behave the way they do, good or bad, overnight. Therefore, parents need to be patient, look for small improvements, and give the consequences time to work.

A final reason is that some parents mistake privileges for rights. Of course, most kids will try to convince their parents that everything is a right. If parents treat privileges as rights, they limit what they can use for consequences. The rights of kids include the right to nourishment, communication with others, clothing, and so on. Watching TV, going out with friends, receiving allowance, using family possessions, are all privileges that can and should be monitored by the parent and used by the child with the parent's approval. The list of rewards in the next chapter will help you identify privileges that can be used as consequences with your children.

Think Ahead

It's wise to set up both positive and negative consequences in advance. For example, when your child does not do her chores, know what negative consequence you plan to use. If your child does what is expected, know what positive consequence you will use. Often, it is helpful to make a general list of consequences for situations or problems that occur frequently. You'll have a chance to do this in the next chapter.

One other thing. Your children should be aware of planned consequences. Don't hesitate to post established consequences, both positive and negative, on your refrigerator door or in your children's rooms. Consequences shouldn't be surprises. In fairness to your kids, they should be aware of what they will get for behaving well or will lose for misbehavior. In our chapter on charts and contracts, we talk about helping your child set and reach reasonable goals. Parents tell us that this also is a good way to spell out positive and negative consequences for their child.

Giving Consequences

Each of the chapters in the following sections of the book outline steps for effectively giving consequences to your child. Until you finish those chapters, these few hints will help you be aware of how your behavior affects the outcome of a consequence. When delivering a consequence, remember to:

1. Be clear. Make sure your child knows what the consequence is and what he or she did to earn or lose it.

2. Be consistent. Don't give a big consequence for a behavior one time and then ignore the same behavior the next time.

3. Be brief. This is especially true with younger children. Clear messages usually get lost when you lecture.

4. Follow through. If you set up a deal for your child to earn a positive consequence, be sure he gets the reward after he's done what he needs to. Likewise, if you give a negative consequence, don't let your child talk you out of it (unless you decide that what you did was totally unreasonable or said out of anger).

5. Be as pleasant as possible. This is generally easier when you give positive consequences. But, when you give negative consequences, keep it in mind, as well. Yelling and screaming are not effective. Kids can't hear your words, they can only hear your anger. Our research tells us that kids are more likely to respond better and learn more from adults who are calm and reasonable, even when giving negative consequences.

Warnings

One last pointer and then it's on to the next chapter. Many parents have fallen prey to warnings—"If you don't stop that, I'll take your game away." Warnings usually do not work and they become a source of frustration for the parents. If you have to come back time after time and deal with the same behavior, you may be talking too much and not giving enough consequences. If you told your child that you would take the game away for a certain misbehavior, and the misbehavior occurs, then take the game away. This helps your child understand what rules are in effect in your family. Otherwise, rules are not only confusing but it becomes a guessing game for your child. "Can I get away with it this time? Mom warned me three times and nothing's happened yet."

Be Confident

It always amazes us how creative and effective parents can be once they learn how to give consequences. All they need is a little push in the right direction and a little confidence that what they are doing will work. In the next two chapters, we will talk about the different types of positive and negative consequences you can use.

Notes

Chapter 4

Positive Consequences

Positive consequences can be a parent's best friend; they are used to increase positive behavior. Positive consequences also can be referred to as rewards. Generally, rewards are things that people like or enjoy. Therefore, when we use the term "reward," we mean any type of consequence that makes behavior occur again.

In the last chapter, the two basic principles you learned are:

- **Negative consequences are used to stop problem behavior.**

- **Positive consequences are used to encourage desirable behavior.**

It's human nature to focus on the negative; just read today's newspaper or watch the evening news. Most stories report negative events. As parents, we sometimes fall into the same trap when it comes to our kids. We focus on their negative behaviors. Kids make mistakes and they don't do everything we'd like them to do. But, they also do many good things. It's to everyone's advantage for parents to focus on what their kids do well.

Using positive consequences is one way to increase the amount of time that kids spend doing positive things. If parents give only negative consequences, they run the risk of becoming a negative consequence themselves. In such situations, children may want to avoid their parents. The alternative is also true. When you give positive consequences, your kids find that spending time with you is more enjoyable. This gives you even more opportunity to use praise and positive consequences.

Parents who balance negative and positive consequences are viewed as more fair and reasonable by their children. (Plus, it's a heck of a lot more fun and rewarding for parents when they give positive consequences.) Parents who consistently use positive consequences are more pleasant and effective and kids are more likely to listen to them.

Bribes

The idea of positive consequences (rewards) is viewed with skepticism by some parents. To them, it seems that kids are being bribed or paid off for doing what they're expected to do. However, rewards are a natural part of daily life. They can range anywhere from obvious things like merit raises at work to subtle things like a smile or a wink. These are given for acceptable behavior—behavior that we want to see again.

Bribery occurs when rewards are given for inappropriate behavior. Giving a child a candy bar to stop him from crying in the grocery store checkout lane is a bribe. (It may seem necessary for our sanity, but it's still a good example of a bribe.) The parent feels forced to do anything to stop the child's negative behavior — "OK, you can have the candy, just shut up!" The child is rewarded for being a brat. If this scenario occurs frequently enough, the result is a child who always wants a reward before he'll act as the parent wants. The reward worked in quieting the kid, but guess what happens the next time the parent is in the checkout lane? Right, crying, and demanding a candy bar. The child has been bribed and wants another bribe before acting appropriately. Therefore, don't give positive consequences for inappropriate behavior—those are bribes. Give rewards for positive behavior.

Positive Consequences That Work

Something that is a reward for one person may not be a reward for someone else. This is sort of like the old saying "different strokes for different folks." Exercise 1 will help you find positive consequences that will work with your

Exercise 1

Activities — What everyday activities does your child like to do? (For example, Nintendo, baseball, watching sitcoms, baking cookies, reading):

First child _____

Second child _____

Possessions — What kinds of material articles does your child like? (For example, sweatshirts, baseball cards, money, dolls, music cassettes):

First child _____

Second child _____

Special activities — What special activities does your child like to do? (For example, going to a ball game, visiting a zoo, going to a movie, having a friend stay overnight):

First child _____

Second child _____

Food – What are your child's favorite foods and beverages? (For example, popcorn, Popsicles, pizza, cola, candy, waffles, granola bars, fruit juice):

First child _____

Second child _____

(NOTE: Do NOT use meals as a negative consequence, for example, taking away a balanced meal and making your child eat bread and water. Children have the right to proper nutrition. In terms of consequences, "Food" refers to special snacks or types of food you can give as rewards.)

People — Who does your child like to spend time with?

First child _____

Second child _____

Attention — What specific kinds of verbal and physical attention from you and others does your child like? (For example, hugs, smiles, compliments, high fives, thumbs up, praise):

First child _____

Second child _____

Other rewards — Is there anything else that your child likes, is interested in, or would like to spend time doing? Is there a favorite chore, or something that he or she has wanted to do but hasn't yet done?

First child _____

Second child _____

child. Using the examples as a guide, identify what your children like to do and write those preferences in the blanks provided. (All parents enjoy consequences that don't cost money. We know you can't run out and buy something every time your child behaves well. Even if you could, it isn't necessarily healthy for your child. In Appendix A, we've included a list of items that are "freebies." Some of these may help you complete the following exercise, also.)

Exercise 1 gives you a list of consequences that can be used to encourage your child's positive behavior. Now, let's look at how to use them.

Pairing Consequences with Behavior

In our chapter on "Effective Praise," we present a method that combines your approval with positive consequences. Also, as a refresher, remember to think about the qualities that make consequences effective (i.e., importance, immediacy, frequency, degree, and contingency). These qualities are important when using positive consequences. The exercise below will help you pair positive consequences with behavior.

Exercise 2 helps prepare you for the upcoming chapter on Effective Praise. In that chapter, we cover how to use the clear message/consequence combination to further encourage your child's desireable behaviors.

Thanks for completing this exercise. The more you use positive consequences, the more likely you are to see positive behavior. Please remember that the most powerful rewards for children can be praise and positive attention from their parents. Keep up the good work. Continue to focus on the positive things your kids do—positive consequences work!

Exercise 2

What positive things do you want your kids to do more often, or more consistently? Use the following list to identify four of those behaviors. Then, assign one of the consequences you have identified to each of those behaviors. Finally, include how much of the consequence you are going to give; for example, one hour of watching TV, a slice of pizza at the mall, etc.

Behavior	Consequence	Amount
1. _____	_____	_____
2. _____	_____	_____
3. _____	_____	_____
4. _____	_____	_____

Chapter 5

Negative Consequences

"I hate you."

"I don't have to do anything I don't want to!"

"I was only an hour late. What's the big deal?"

"But, why do I have to clean my room? None of my friends clean theirs."

OK, so you won't give positive consequences for all behaviors. Kids are going to say and do things we don't like. We all realize kids are going to misbehave. When they do, they should receive negative consequences. If the consequences are given in a firm, fair, and consistent manner, they will be effective (and so will you).

As a parent, your first goal should be to find what negative consequences work. Just like with positive consequences, different negative consequences are effective with some kids and not with others. One key to look for when determining the effectiveness of a consequence is the result—did the negative behavior stop or occur less often?

We will concentrate on using two forms of negative consequences—taking away a privilege for misbehavior (for example, the list of positive consequences you made in the last chapter) and adding work in the area of the misbehavior (vacuuming the carpet after tracking dirt in).

Removing Positive Consequences

When a problem behavior occurs, one type of negative consequence is the removal of a privilege. Some situations are tailor-made for this. For example, if your teen comes home an hour late, you may remove part of the privilege (coming home an hour earlier next time she goes out),

or if this is a frequent problem, she may lose the privilege of going out altogether. Similarly, if your two kids are arguing about which TV show to watch, you can shut off the TV until they settle their differences, or they could lose TV for the rest of the evening.

Using the method that we presented in Chapter 2, you can combine clear messages with negative consequences. You could say to your teenager, "Sarah, you're one hour late. As a result, you can't go out tomorrow night." To your two kids arguing over the TV, you could say, "Bob and Ray, you're arguing about which show to watch. Please shut the TV off until you can calmly come to me with a solution."

Always keep in mind the qualities that make consequences effective. In deciding what consequence to use, you would ask the following:

Was the consequence:

Important? — Does Sarah really like to go out?

Immediate? — Did you give the consequence right away?

Frequent? — Has she lost the privilege of going out so often that she doesn't really care any more?

The right amount? — Was losing one night out with her friends enough (or too much of) a consequence?

Contingent? — Did you use Grandma's Rule? "If you come home on time tonight, you can earn the privilege of going out tomorrow night."

Exercise 1

Now, identify some of your child's problem behaviors. Then list the negative consequence (removal of privileges) you would use in each situation.

Behavior	Consequence	Amount
Example:		
Didn't do homework	No TV	For the rest of the night
1. _____	_____	_____
2. _____	_____	_____
3. _____	_____	_____
4. _____	_____	_____

Adding Work

This is an effective method for teaching responsibility. It takes time and effort from your child to correct the problem, time that he could spend playing or doing something fun. Many times, the consequence relates directly to the problem; in fact, the consequence actually is designed to "make up" for the misbehavior. Other times, simply by adding a chore you provide a negative consequence. So, instead of removing a privilege, you're having your child do something constructive to get your message across.

The process of adding work is simple. For example, if your son constantly leaves his clothes laying on the floor, he must pick them up before he gets to do what he wants to do. Or he must gather the dirty clothes from every family member and put them in the hamper. Adding work is another way of teaching responsibility.

Examples

- Your daughter breaks a friend's toy. To teach her responsibility, she must use part of her weekly allowance to buy a new toy.

- Your son throws his clean clothes in a wadded-up ball in the corner of his closet. He must fold those clothes as well as help you fold the next load of laundry.

- Your daughter borrows the car and returns it on time. However, the car is dirty, and there are numerous food and candy wrappers inside. She wants to call her best friend and talk to her. You decide that she is to wash the car and clean out the inside before she can make the call.

- Your son doesn't get the trash to the curb on time. You put him in charge of emptying all of the wastebaskets inside the house for the next week.

- Your son and daughter are fighting about who last put away the clean dishes. To help them learn how to get along, you have them rake and bag the leaves in the front yard.

Exercise 2

In the following situations, decide how you would correct your child by adding work:

1. **Your daughter left a mess on the dining room table.**

   _____

   _____

2. **Your son jumped on a chair. It fell over and broke a lamp.**

   _____

   _____

3. **Your daughter left a pan of soup on the stove and it boiled over, making a mess on the stove.**

   _____

   _____

4. **Your son tells you he left his books at school so he can't do his homework.**

   _____

5. **Your daughter and son argue over who has to set the table.**

   _____

Giving Negative Consequences

The effectiveness of your consequences depends, in part, on how you give them. An angry response by you is not going to work; it may even result in more problems. Our experience tells us that kids respond better and learn more from adults who are pleasant and positive, even when they are giving negative consequences.

With that in mind, refer to our chapter on Corrective Teaching for a method to give negative consequences. Parents have found that Corrective Teaching gives them a formula for using consequences to deal with routine negative behavior.

Are You Giving a Negative Consequence?

Sometimes, parents make the mistake of assuming that a consequence is negative. We encourage parents to look at the effect of the consequence on the behavior they want to change. If the behavior stops or decreases in frequency, you've given a negative consequence. If the behavior continues or occurs more often, you've given a positive consequence. For example, one mother told us that her 6-year-old continually fidgeted and talked in church. She told him that he couldn't come with her next time if he continued causing problems in church. Sure enough, that kid fidgeted like crazy and talked more than ever. He didn't want to be in church to begin with! His mother's "negative consequence" actually encouraged more problem behaviors. The behavior she wanted to stop actually increased. She gave him a positive consequence.

Without going into too much detail, we told her to do one of the following:

1. **Remove a privilege** — he couldn't play with his friend after church. Or,

2. **Use Grandma's Rule** — if he sits quietly,

the family can stop for ice cream on the way home after church.

Actually, the mother used both methods. And, they worked. The young boy learned to sit quietly in church.

Pay close attention to the effect a negative consequence has on the behavior you want to change. If the problem behavior has decreased or ended altogether, you gave an effective consequence.

The Snowball Effect

One problem with negative consequences is that parents can lose sight of when to stop. If one consequence doesn't work, parents often try another that is harsher. This can lead to an upward spiral where the parent ends up grounding the child for the next five years, or something totally off the wall like that. Usually, this happens when parents are frustrated and upset. Children know what buttons to push, and parents can quickly lose their patience. That's when the snowball effect usually takes place.

For example, Amy didn't clean her room so her dad took away her telephone privileges for a weekend. Her room was messy the next day. For this, she lost a week of TV privileges. The room didn't get any cleaner, so her dad added another month without phone privileges, another week without TV, and told her that she couldn't come out of her room until it was spotless.

Whew! This wasn't just the snowball effect; this became an avalanche! In three days, this girl lost just about all communication with the outside world! This was a good example of getting carried away with ineffective negative consequences. Instead of repeating negative consequences in rapid-fire succession, step back and look at the effects of the consequence on the behavior. Change the consequence if necessary, but don't continue to pile consequence on consequence. More is not necessarily better. Since the consequences given by this father were unreasonable, we suggested that he go back, talk to Amy, and set up the following plan:

1. He helps Amy clean her room.

2. In return, Amy helps him clean the garage.

If these two parts of the plan were completed, Amy could have her privileges back. To help Amy keep the room clean consistently, we helped him find a way to put Grandma's Rule into practice—each day that Amy cleans her room, she gets to use the phone and watch her favorite TV show. This practical solution worked. Amy's room was not spotless, but it was clean much more often than it was dirty. And, Dad knew exactly what consequence he would use whether the room was clean or dirty. Dad learned how to avoid the snowball effect and still give a negative consequence that worked.

It helps when parents are willing to look at their own behavior. They need to determine if they are giving too many negative consequences or if the consequences are too extreme. If you find out that you are going overboard when giving negative consequences, alter them. Remember, the correction needs to fit the behavior.

One consequence that works well with younger children is "Time-Out." For a description of how to use "Time-Out," see Appendix B.

For those of you with older children and teens, Appendix C is a list of chores you can use for minor and major problem behaviors.

Finding effective negative consequences is a challenge for parents, but it is not impossible. If your children misbehave, do one of the following — remove all or part of a privilege, or add work. Be logical, fair, and consistent and you're on the road to using effective consequences.

Notes _____
_____
_____
_____
_____
_____
_____
_____
_____
_____
_____

Encouraging Positive Behaviors

Chapter 6

Effective Praise

Praise is powerful. Praising your child is one of the most important things you can do as a parent.

Praise is nourishment. It helps your child grow emotionally, just as food helps your child grow physically. Praise is nourishment for your child's mind and self-esteem.

Focus on the Positive

Praise is not a new concept; we're all familiar with it. But many of us don't use it as often as we should. Why? One of the reasons is that we have been trained to see negatives. It is easy to see what people do wrong. Some companies operate their businesses on what they call the 3:11 rule. For example, if you go to a restaurant and have a good meal, you'll probably tell three other people about it. On the other hand, if you get a lousy meal, you'll probably tell eleven other people! Think about it, isn't that focusing on the negative?

Parents often focus on the negative, too. It's easy for them to see the mistakes and shortcomings of their children. None of us need to look very far to find something wrong.

At Boys Town, we have found one thing to be true time and time again—praise works wonders. When parents use praise, kids change dramatically. When parents "zero in" on as many positive things as they can, kids feel better about themselves.

Some parents tell us that they praise their children, but it just doesn't seem to work. Usually, we find that these parents only praise outstanding achievements or momentous occasions. We tell them to look for little things to praise, also. After parents begin praising small improvements, they notice many positive changes in their kids' behavior. This is not coincidence. Praise works.

Other parents ask, "Why should I praise my kids for something that they're supposed to do?" Good question. We answer them with another question. "Do you like being recognized for the things you do well, regardless of whether you're supposed to do them? Do you like to hear your boss tell you what a good job you're doing?" Most parents say "Of course." And then add, "And, I wouldn't mind hearing it a little more often." Enough said. We all like to hear about things we do well.

When praising your kids, it helps to look closely at three areas:

1. **Things your kids already do well** (and maybe you take for granted).

2. **Improvements**, even small improvements, in problem areas.

3. **Positive attempts at new skills**.

For example, praise your kids for being up on time, or cleaning their rooms, or turning off their lights if you haven't mentioned your appreciation for a long time. Most likely, they will continue to do these things since you took the time to notice.

If your kids try hard to learn something new, praise the effort. Praise any step in the right direction. Learning a skill requires learning small parts of it, then putting all of the steps together. When your child was learning to walk, you probably praised each and every improvement—from first standing alone, to taking that first awkward step, to finally putting a series of steps together. You praised positive attempts at a new skill. You praised improvements. This level of enthusiasm and the same attention to trying can carry over to many areas of your children's lives, regardless of age—riding a bike, driving a car, talking with guests, making friends, and so on. Seize every opportunity to recognize positive attempts to learn.

The easiest way to praise someone is to say things like, "Fantastic," "Great," or "Keep up the good work." This is a good start; however, we suggest you take it a little further to make sure your child receives a clear message. That's why we make a distinction between praise, in general, and what we call "Effective Praise."

Effective Praise allows you to:

- Recognize your children sincerely and enthusiastically for the progress they are making;

- Specifically describe what you like;

- Give a reason why you like it.

In the chapter on "Clear Messages," we talked about a framework to use when teaching your children. This is the basis for Effective Praise:

1. **Show your approval.** Smiling and touching are enthusiastic ways to show approval. A brief praise statement is also effective.

2. **Describe the positive**. Give clear, specific descriptions of what your child did well.

3. **Give a reason**. Tell how that behavior helps your child, or why that behavior is appreciated by others.

Consistently using Effective Praise will result in more positive behaviors from your children. Consistently "catching 'em being good" results in kids who like themselves and grow in self-confidence.

Let's look at an example of Effective Praise. Your teenage son just called to tell you where he was.

Show your approval — "Thanks for calling me."

Describe the positive — "I'm really glad that you let me know where you were and why you'll be a little late."

Give a reason — "Calling me shows a lot of sensitivity and shows that I can trust you."

In this brief scenario, your child learned specifically what he did right and why it was so important. You increased the likelihood that he will call the next time he's out.

Let's look at these relatively easy steps and see why they are important.

Show Your Approval

Kids are like the rest of us. They not only like to hear nice things said about them, but they'll also work harder to get more praise in the future. When you combine a sign of your approval with specific praise, the praise is that much more meaningful.

There are numerous words that show your approval. And, for goodness sakes, show a little excitement!

Awesome!... Terrific!... Wow!... You're right on target!... I love you... I'm impressed!... Super!... Amazing!... That's great!... Wonderful!... Magnificent!...Excellent!... (Doesn't it make you feel better just saying these words?)

There also are numerous actions that convey your approval:

Hugging them...Kissing them...Picking them up... Winking or smiling at them ... Giving them a "thumbs up" or an A-OK sign... Ruffling their hair...Giving them "five"...Nodding your head... Clapping for them...

Showing your approval lets kids know that you're excited about what they're doing. Every kid gives us something to be happy about. Every kid does something that deserves praise. Let's make sure we recognize it, and most of all, let's tell them.

Describe the Positive

After you have given a praise statement, describe the specific behaviors you liked. Make sure your kids understand what they did so that they can repeat the behavior in the future. Give them clear messages. Praise what you just saw or heard your child do well. For example, "Sue, thanks for cleaning the dishes and helping me put the leftovers away." Or, "Eddie, I'm glad you washed your hands after you went to the bathroom."

Remember to use words your kids understand. Make it brief and to the point. Just let your child know what was done well.

Give a Reason

Children benefit from knowing why a behavior is helpful to them or others. It helps them understand the relationship between their behavior and what happens to them.

For example, if your teenager volunteers to clean up the family room before guests come over (and then does it), explain why that behavior is helpful. For example, "Cleaning the family room really saved us a lot of time. We have time to get everything finished before guests come over."

You could give lots of reasons why helping out benefits your teen. Some others are: "Helping others is a real plus. If you do that on the job, your boss is more likely to give you a raise."

"Since you helped out, I'll have time to take you over to your friend's house when you wanted to go. I don't know if I would have had time if you hadn't helped."

Exercise 1

In the exercises listed below, give reasons for the following statements:

1. **It's important to answer the phone politely because...** _____

_____

_____

2. **It's important not to make excuses to your teacher because...** _____

_____

_____

3. **Drive the car without listening to your Walkman because...** _____

_____

_____

4. **Picking up your things is important because...** _____

_____

_____

5. **Sharing your toys with others is helpful because...** _____

_____

_____

Giving your child a reason shows the relationship between his or her behavior and the consequences or outcomes. Reasons are particularly valuable when they can demonstrate the benefits your child may receive, either immediately or in the future. The reasons should be brief, believable, and age-appropriate.

Here are some reasons that other parents gave that may be helpful with your child:

1. It's important to answer the phone politely because it will give the caller a good impression.

2. It's important not to make excuses to your teacher because it looks like you're not taking responsibility for your homework.

3. Drive the car without listening to your Walkman because you'll be able to hear important sounds—like a siren from a police car or ambulance.

4. Picking up your things is important because people won't step on them.

5. Sharing your toys with others is helpful because they're more likely to share their toys with you.

Optional Reward

Occasionally, you may want to add a fourth step to Effective Praise—a reward. When you are especially pleased with a certain behavior, or your child has made a big improvement in a certain area, you can reward your child with a special privilege. (Refer back to the list you made in the "Positive Consequences" chapter for privileges or activities you can use.)

Rewards can be big or small, that's up to you. Just as long as it fits the behavior you want to encourage.

Let's take a look at some examples of Effective Praise:

> *Show Approval* — "Michael, that's great!"
>
> *Describe Positive* — "You tied your tennis shoes all by yourself!"
>
> *Give Reason* — "Now, you won't have to wait for me to do it for you."

Show Approval—"I'm so proud of you!"

Describe Positive — "You did your homework before watching TV."

Give Reason — "Now, you won't have to do it late at night."

Optional Reward — "You're sure welcome to some popcorn while you watch the movie."

Show Approval — "Kathy, what a nice job!"

Describe Positive — "The people you babysat for called and said they were so pleased with way you played with their kids and got them to bed on time."

Give Reason — "They told me that because you were so responsible, they wanted you to babysit next Saturday night, too."

Notes

Exercise 2

Think of four things your kids did that deserved praise. In the spaces below, use the steps of Effective Praise to practice what you would say to your children.

1. Show Approval _____

_____

_____

Describe Positive _____

_____

_____

Give Reason _____

_____

_____

2. Show Approval _____

_____

_____

Describe Positive _____

_____

_____

Give Reason _____

_____

_____

3. Show Approval _____

_____

_____

Describe Positive _____

_____

_____

Give Reason _____

_____

_____

4. Show Approval _____

_____

_____

Describe Positive _____

_____

_____

Give Reason _____

_____

_____

One final note. In interviews with some of the thousands who have completed our parenting classes, parents have consistently told us that Effective Praise has had a lasting impact on their families. Parents find themselves being more positive about their kids. Kids, in turn, are more positive about their parents. With Effective Praise, everyone wins.

Chapter 7

Preventive Teaching

Ben Franklin once said, "An ounce of prevention is worth a pound of cure." Old Ben was right; society's reliance on preventive measures is proof of that. We have fire drills; we have our cars tuned up; we go to the doctor for a physical exam. We do all of these precautionary things to prevent problems. While practicing a fire drill may not keep a fire from starting, it could prevent a catastrophe such as the loss of life in a fire. Prevention is both necessary and important.

An Ounce of Prevention

We've taken Ben's wisdom and applied it to parenting. We call our method "Preventive Teaching." Preventive Teaching is our "ounce of prevention." We, as parents, can spend time teaching skills *before* our kids need to use them. We can help our kids prevent problems from occurring. When children know what is expected of them, and have the opportunity to prepare, they will be more successful.

You've probably used Preventive Teaching many times before—teaching your child how to safely cross the street, what number to dial in case of emergency, what clothes to wear when it's cold, and so on. Preventive Teaching helps you anticipate and prevent problems while setting your child up for success. Preventive Teaching is *teaching your child what he or she will need to know for a future situation and practicing it in advance.*

There are two specific times that you can use Preventive Teaching:

1. **When your child is learning something new.**

2. **When your child has had difficulty in a past situation.**

Of course, the Preventive Teaching areas you focus on will vary with each child, but all kids can learn something new or improve behaviors that have caused problems in the past. You may want your young child to learn how to make his own breakfast or how to answer the phone. You may want him to improve in areas where he has had difficulties before, like playing nicely with others or getting to bed on time. For a young teen, you may want to teach how to ask (or refuse) a date or how to drive a car. You may want him to improve in situations where he loses his temper or doesn't know how to respond to a teacher. (Please go to the next page and do Exercise 1 now.)

Preventive Teaching helps you take care of these situations and increase the likelihood that your child will do well. It's a simple concept, but parents usually don't use it as often or in as many situations as they could. Here are some examples of how other parents have used Preventive Teaching. These parents taught their children how to:

- Come in from playing when called

- Ask for make-up work in school

- Apologize for getting in a fight

- Say "No" if someone offers alcohol

- Sit quietly and not ask for candy in the store

Exercise 1

Think of areas in which your child needs to learn something new. List these in the following spaces:

1. _____

_____

2. _____

_____

3. _____

_____

Think of areas in which your child has had difficulties and needs to improve. List these in the following spaces:

1. _____

_____

2. _____

_____

3. _____

_____

- Accept buying the "sale" jeans
- Accept a "No" answer

Let's look closely at each step of Preventive Teaching.

Describe What You Would Like

Before your children can do what you want, they must first know what it is that you expect. Break the skill down into specific steps. Make sure your children understand. For example, if your daughter argued with the referee at her last soccer game, you would teach her how to respond before her next game. You might say, "Sharon, tonight at the soccer game, you need to remain calm if the referee makes a call against you or your team. Try keeping your mouth closed, taking a deep breath, and walking toward your coach when you get upset."

Give a Reason

Children, like adults, benefit from knowing why they should act a certain way. Reasons explain to a child why new skills and appropriate behaviors are helpful and important. They also teach how inappropriate behaviors are harmful. The best reasons, of course, are those that relate directly to the person's life. Simply saying to your kids, "Do it because I said so," is a command, not a reason. It does not give your kids any relationship between their actions and future benefits to them.

Sometimes it is difficult to come up with reasons that mean a lot to your kids at that time. Even if they don't immediately agree with what you are saying, at least they will know why you think it is important. That means a great deal since reasons are indications of fairness and logic. Kids are much more likely to comply with what you say when you give reasons. If reasons are personal to the youth, they are more likely to accept what you are teaching. For example, "When you yell or get upset with the referee, it takes your mind off of the game and you don't play as well."

Practice

Knowing what to do and how to do it are two different things. Any new skill needs to be practiced. You can tell your child how to ride a bicycle, but that hardly will ensure that she could hop right on and take off. It takes practice to become good at almost anything.

Children occasionally are reluctant to practice—especially when being taught a new skill.

They may feel embarrassed, or lack the self-confidence, or think that practicing is a waste of time. The fact of the matter is that practice actually eases embarrassment and raises self-confidence in their abilities. If you are enthusiastic about practicing, your kids will be more willing to practice. Encourage them as they practice and use a lot of praise for trying. Most practices should be fun, yet realistic. This isn't the time to be ultra-serious or the practice will become drudgery for you and your child.

In the previous example, you were teaching your daughter how to stay calm after a referee's call. When it's time for practice, you might say, "OK, Sharon, pretend I'm the referee and I've just called a foul on you. Show me what you'll do to stay calm. OK?"

Practice is so important to kids who are learning skills. And, it can be an enjoyable time with your children—especially when they understand that you are practicing because you care about them.

Praise areas that your child did well in and encourage your child to improve in areas that need improvement. Don't expect perfection the first time you practice. You can practice again if you need to. Or, you can practice later on in the day.

If you are practicing a complex skill or a difficult situation, such as how to say "No" to peer pressure and using drugs, never promise that the real situation will work out perfectly. Stress to your child that you are practicing possible ways to handle a situation and the outcome won't always be the same. This is no different than what we go through in our daily lives. We know that a certain method of dealing with one person won't work with another person. As a parent, remember that you cannot ensure your child's success in every situation; you can only improve the odds. Your kids will learn that every situation is different, but they won't be defenseless. You will help them learn more and more ways to solve problems, until they have a repertoire of solutions.

After finishing any teaching situation, it is wise to *encourage future use*. A few words of encouragement can motivate your child to use what he or she has learned in real situations. As your child learns, it will not be necessary to go through each step of Preventive Teaching.

Notes

Preventive Prompts

Experience adds skills and when your child is faced with similar situations, you may just provide a reminder—a preventive prompt. For example, let's say that you have practiced with your daughter on how to stay calm when she gets upset with her friends. You could say, "Remember, Sharon, stay calm just like we practiced for your soccer games. Don't say anything and take a few deep breaths. Then walk away from them if you have to."

Then, just before your daughter goes out to play with her friends, you could give a preventive prompt: "Remember what we practiced, Sharon. You'll do just fine." The purpose of a preventive prompt is to get your child focused on what you have practiced. Your praise and encouragement during the whole Preventive Teaching sequence will help your child remember important skills to use.

Let's look at some examples of Preventive Teaching:

Your son is about to go outside to play and has had difficulty coming in when he's called.

Describe what you want
"Robbie, when I call you to come in for dinner, let me know that you heard me and pick up your toys before coming in right away."

Give a reason
"If you come in right away, you'll have a better chance of having time to play after dinner."

Practice
"Let's pretend I've just called you in. What are you going to say and do? ...Great! Now run and have fun. Remember to come home right away when I call."

Your teenage daughter is going to a party with some friends and you want to help her be prepared if anyone offers her an alcoholic beverage.

Describe what you want
"We've talked about this before, Lori, but it's real important so I just want to go over it again before you go out tonight. Do you remember what you can say if someone offers you something to drink?"

Lori — "Yeah, mom. I should say, 'I won't drink because my parents would ground me. I wouldn't get to go out next week.'"

"Great! And if they kept pestering you?"

Lori — "I could say, 'I like you guys but if you keep bugging me about drinking, I'm just going to leave—I'm not going to drink, OK?'"

Give a reason
"Lori, I know that sometimes it's tough, but letting your friends know that you won't drink will help you stay out of trouble. Not only is drinking illegal, it's also dangerous. So as long as you stay away from drinking and drugs, I'll be more likely to let you go out with friends, OK?"

Practice
(In this situation you've already had her practice saying what she would say to her friends so another practice here would not be necessary.)

Now go to Page 41 and complete Exercise 2.

Preventive Teaching is a valuable tool for both parents and children. By using it with your children, you can promote gradual behavior changes in areas where they may be having problems and help them prepare for unfamiliar situations. Preventive Teaching can increase your children's self-esteem by showing them that *they* can learn how to change their behaviors and avoid problems. And, perhaps most importantly, Preventive Teaching allows you and your child to work toward goals together. Taking the time to be with your children and showing them that you care helps improve relationships, and that benefits the whole family.

Exercise 2

Think of three situations in which you can use Preventive Teaching. In the spaces below, use the steps of Preventive Teaching to write what you would say to your child.

1. **Describe what you want** _____

   _____

   Give a reason _____

   _____

   Practice _____

   _____

2. **Describe what you want** _____

   _____

   Give a reason _____

   _____

   Practice _____

   _____

3. **Describe what you want** _____

   _____

   Give a reason _____

   _____

   Practice _____

   _____

Chapter 8

Developing Family Rules

All families have rules. Most of the time, these are unwritten expectations for parents and children. For example, one family's unwritten rule is, "Everyone gets their own breakfast in the morning." Another family's unwritten rule is, "If you mess something up, you clean it up." Now, these rules have never been written down. But they are still rules these families follow.

The difficulty comes when rules aren't clear. That leads to family members living by different sets of rules. If your rules aren't clear your children may be living by one set of rules while you live by another. For example, you think that your kids should be getting themselves up at 7 a.m. and you feel frustrated when they don't. They think that you should get them up. This is just the first of many daily examples where vague family rules end up being confusing and frustrating for parents and kids. In this chapter we'll discuss how to clarify family rules and how to use a format for making new rules.

The first step in developing a set of family rules is identifying unwritten rules you already use.

Here are some examples of rules from other parents.

Rules for Older Children

1. When you complete all your homework and have it checked, you may watch TV or use the phone.

2. When you study or read at least one hour on Sunday through Thursday nights, you get to go out on Friday or Saturday night.

Exercise 1

In the space below, write some of the rules that are used in your family.

1. _____

   _____

2. _____

   _____

3. _____

   _____

4. _____

   _____

5. _____

   _____

3. When you want to go out on the weekends, ask at least two days in advance (Wednesday for Friday, Thursday for Saturday).

4. In order to use the car, ask at least one day in advance. Bring it back with the same amount of gas, and be willing to wash it when we think it is necessary.

5. Please limit your phone calls to four 15-minute calls a night. All calls end before 10 o'clock.

6. Before asking to go anywhere or do anything, complete all housework (make bed, clean room, put clothes where they belong) and school work.

7. If you disagree with an answer, disagree calmly without arguing. Then we will listen to you. When you argue you will lose 15 minutes or more of your curfew.

8. Check with us to make sure there are no family plans before making your own. Then you will know whether you will be able to attend your activity.

9. Before going out, be prepared to answer questions like: Where are you going? What are you going to do? Who will you be with? When do you plan to be back?

Rules for Younger Children

1. Keep your feet off the furniture so you don't lose any of your play time.

2. When you come home, hang your coat where it belongs and put your shoes in your closet; then you may have a snack.

3. Everyone cleans their plate and puts it in the sink before dessert is served.

4. When you do something nice for someone else in the family at least once each day, you will not get a chore after dinner.

5. Bedtime is at 8:30 p.m. and we start getting ready at 7:30. If you are ready for bed by 8 o'clock, we'll have time to read a story.

6. Say your prayers before each meal and before going to bed.

7. If you ask permission before you turn on the TV, you will be more likely to get to watch what you want.

8. Flush the toilet and wash your hands after you go to the bathroom.

9. Before sitting down to the dinner table, be sure to wash your hands.

These rules have three qualities that make them useful:

1. **Each rule includes a clear message**; that way your child understands what needs to be done. Make sure your rules are simple enough to be followed.

2. **Each rule is stated in the positive**. They tell a child what to do, instead of what *not* to do. Therefore, your children try to do something good rather than avoid doing something bad.

3. **Most rules include or imply a consequence**. (Rules 6, 8, and 9 for Younger Children are some of the rules that do not specify a consequence.) When you spell out the consequence in a rule, your children know what they can expect if they follow it.

Use these qualities when you put together your own family rules. Get your kids involved. When they have problems that involve other members of the family, take time to discuss possible solutions with everyone in the family. If these solutions look like they can apply to all family members, make them into family rules.

Making Your Own Family Rules

Here are the steps for developing rules for your family:

1. Think of what rules you want and why.

You've already done some of this with the exercise earlier in this chapter. Now is a time to think of other changes you might like to see. Make rules that everyone in the family can follow. First of all, make sure that you can follow up with any consequences promised in the rule. Second, lead by example. If you expect your kids to get their clothes in the hamper each morning, put yours there, too.

Make sure your expectations are reasonable for your child's age and abilities. For example, a rule stating that everyone should make their bed each day is reasonable as long as you understand that your 4-year-old won't be able to do it exactly right. There will probably be wrinkled sheets and one or two stuffed animals under the blanket. On the other hand, your 13-year-old should be able to make the bed without any problems.

2. Decide on rules for your family.

Discuss family rules with your children. It's a good idea to see what rules they think currently exist. Your kids will have ideas for additional rules, and that's good. They are more likely to follow rules they help make.

Make sure that your rules are specific. For example, "Keep your phone calls short," is a vague rule. A short phone call to your 16-year-old may seem like a lifetime to you. Instead, "You can talk on the phone 3 times a night for 15 minutes each time," is a clear rule that everyone can understand.

Once you have clear, reasonable rules, write them down and post them in a convenient location. Many families put their rules on the refrigerator, knowing that everyone will see them there.

3. Include positive and negative consequences.

The rule "When you complete all homework and have it checked, you may watch TV," includes a positive consequence for completing homework and having it checked – your child gets to watch TV. It also implies that if you don't complete your homework and don't have it checked, you cannot watch TV. By including the consequence in the rule, it is clear to everyone what will happen if they do or don't follow the rule.

On the other hand, some rules purposely don't have clear consequences. For example, the rule "Wash your hands before each meal" implies that if you don't wash your hands, you'll have to wash them before dinner. It may not be necessary to have any more of a consequence with this rule unless it is a frequent problem. In general though, it's more helpful to you and your kids if consequences are included with rules.

4. Review when necessary.

When you find that everyone regularly follows a rule or a rule doesn't work very well, it's time to review the need for that rule. Family meetings are a great place to do this review. Family meetings also provide time for everyone to have a say in any new rules. When you have new rules, it's a good idea to review them in one or two weeks to see how well they work.

Having family rules is one more way of encouraging positive behavior in your children. Specifying family rules can produce dramatic changes. Your home runs smoother and all family members are happier when they know exactly what is expected of them.

Notes _____

_____

_____

_____

_____

_____

_____

_____

_____

_____

_____

_____

_____

_____

_____

_____

_____

_____

_____

_____

_____

_____

_____

_____

Responding
to Problem Behaviors

Chapter 9

Staying Calm

Many parents tell us that the biggest challenge they face in dealing with their child's problem behaviors is staying calm. We all know there are times our kids are going to make us upset and angry. Kids can be sarcastic, defiant, rebellious, and possibly violent. Parents have to prepare themselves for times like these and learn to keep their cool.

Please understand that we are not saying you won't get angry. That's impossible, maybe even unhealthy, since anger is a basic human emotion. We are simply saying that blowing your top over your child's behavior can make situations worse. The way we look at it, anger is only one letter away from "danger." Our experience tells us that staying calm and controlling angry responses is much more effective in teaching kids how to behave.

The First Step

Knowing what makes us angry is the first step in being able to respond calmly to our kids' problem behaviors. When we ask other parents what they do when they are angry, they typically say they yell or cuss at their kids. Some say that they hit something, and throw or kick things. Many parents were totally convinced that these angry responses worked. And they were right. These responses did temporarily stop the problem behavior. But, what did their children learn? To yell or hit, to throw or kick things when they are upset.

As these parents went through our *Common Sense Parenting* classes, they learned to stay calm in tense situations. And, they reported the following results:

1. The temper tantrum or problem behavior **stopped sooner**.

2. The behavior **did not last as long** and **wasn't as severe**.

3. The **parent felt better** about the way he or she handled the situation.

In one particular case, a stepparent told us, "You know, that 'calm' thing really works. My son used to run away frequently. And I didn't handle the situation too well. I lost my temper each time. After I learned how to stay calm and not go bonkers, we *both* stayed more calm and were able to work things out without him running away."

Of course, staying calm was just one of the effective changes this man made in his parenting style. But staying calm was the first step. He learned that all of those other times, his anger got in the way of what he wanted to teach his stepson. As he learned to remain calm, he was able to put his other parenting skills to work. This made a dramatic, positive change in the relationship between this man and his stepson.

Calming Down

Staying calm wasn't easy for this parent, at first. He had to work at it. Here are some ways that other parents have told us that they calm down in tense situations.

• "I count to ten—very slowly. I concentrate

Exercise 1

What do your kids do that makes you downright angry? List three of these behaviors on the following lines.

1. _____

   _____

2. _____

   _____

3. _____

   _____

What do you do in response to these behaviors? Write those in the blanks provided.

1. _____

   _____

2. _____

   _____

3. _____

   _____

on doing that regardless of what my son is yelling."

- "I put my hands in my pockets. I tend to be really demonstrative with my hands, especially when I'm angry. Before I learned to do this, I think my daughter thought I was going to hit her. I wasn't, but she viewed my behavior as a threat."

- "I sit down. If I'm standing, I begin to tremble. Sitting calms me for some reason. I can still tell my child what he's doing wrong, but I say it a lot more calmly."

- "I take a deep breath and let it out slowly. This kind of serves as a safety valve to me. It's like I'm letting steam out of my body."

- "I just leave the situation for awhile. I go in another room until I can handle myself. I figure if my kid's that mad, taking a little time to regain my control won't hurt anything. I can deal with it a lot better that way. Sometimes, he even calms down by the time I get back."

- "This may sound crazy, but I wear a rubber band on my wrist and snap the band whenever I feel like I'm getting upset. That's a signal to myself that I'd better calm down."

- "I used to get so upset with my 15-year-old that I would have to go outside for a walk to calm down. I couldn't do this everytime, but it's been helpful on many occasions."

- "I call someone like my best friend or my sister. By talking about the situation, I can go back in and deal with it more calmly."

- "I sit down and on paper write about how upset I am. Sometimes, I can't even read what I've written. That's not as important as the fact that I'm not taking it out on him. When I calm down, I'm always surprised at how upset I got at such a little thing."

So far, we've talked about ways to calm down when you're angry. One other suggestion is to calm down as soon as you recognize you're getting angry—before reaching your boiling point.

What do you do now when trying to stay calm? Use Exercise 2 to make a record of your methods.

Exercise 2

Do you have any methods of anger control that work for you? If you do, please list them on the following lines:

1. _____

   _____

2. _____

   _____

3. _____

   _____

Exercise 3

Please take a few minutes and think about the little signals that your body gives off to tell you you're getting angry. List them in the following spaces:

1. _____

2. _____

3. _____

4. _____

We all have little signals that warn us that we're getting angry. Recognizing these signals allows us to think before we act. It's much easier to find a solution to a problem when you're calm. This next exercise will help you recognize these signals.

Listed below are some ways people react or feel when they start to get angry.

- Tight muscles
- Sweating
- Speak faster
- Face feels flush
- Grind or clench teeth
- Heart pounds
- Lips quiver when you speak
- Ringing in your ears
- Tremble or shake

Now, let's take a look at how you can use these signals to help you stay calm in tense situations with your children. Here's how we taught other parents to put this information in practice. What we're going to do in this example is combine:

1. our child's problem behaviors, and

2. our early warning signals, with

3. a way of staying calm that works for us.

Use this information to prepare yourself for the next time you are upset with your child's behavior.

Example

The next time Johnny *talks back to me and refuses to go to bed*, (child's problem behaviors), and I start *feeling my heart pound*, (my warning signals) *I will take a deep breath and let it out slowly before I correct him* (what I will do to stay calm).

Staying calm is tough. But, parents tell us it's the most important part of being successful in teaching their kids. You may have to work at it; some parents tell us it was the most difficult skill they had to learn. But, you will find as they have, that the benefits are well worth the effort.

Exercise 4

Now, take some time to prepare a similar plan for yourself. We have found that when parents write out their plan, they are more likely to remember and use it during a real situation.

The next time my child

_____
(child's problem behaviors)
and I start

_____
(my warning signals)
I will

_____
(what I will do to stay calm)

Tips

Learning to control your negative reactions will take some time. Don't get discouraged if you lose your temper every now and then. Here are some tips that have helped other parents:

1. **Don't take what your child says personally**. This may be very difficult when your child is calling you every name in the book. But remember, your child hasn't yet acquired the skills necessary to deal with anger or frustration. Don't react when you get called a name or when you are accused of being a rotten parent. Learn how to let negative, angry comments bounce off you and the effectiveness of your teaching will increase.

2. Another method that works for most parents is the "take five" rule. Instead of blurting out an angry response, **tell yourself to take five minutes to think about what is happening**. It is remarkable how that "cooling off" period can help a person regain self-control and put things in perspective. Simply leaving the situation can help to "defuse" a volatile situation.

3. **Focus on behavior instead of what you think the reasons are for your child's misbehavior**. Don't look for motives; instead, deal with the way your child is acting. You can drive yourself batty trying to figure out reasons for your child's negative behavior. After the problem is solved, then take the time to talk to your child about what happened and why.

4. **If you get angry and say or do something you regret, go back and say that you're sorry**. This teaches your kids how to behave when they make a mistake. Apologize, say what you did wrong, and what you're going to do differently next time. (Some parents worry about apologizing to their kids because they think they lose some of their parental control. We've found apologizing helps kids realize that we all, young and old alike, make mistakes. The best thing is to admit it and do your best not to let it happen again.)

5. Staying calm does not mean you are totally passive. **There are times when you will raise your voice—but it is a firm, no-nonsense voice tone**. And, the words you use are specific descriptions, not judgments or feelings. Staying calm means you don't react to misbehavior in an angry, aggressive manner.

In summary:

1. Stay calm.

2. Look at your own behavior.

3. Identify what makes you angry.

4. Know what you are going to say and do.

5. Control negative responses and deal with them quickly.

6. Your own self-control is a key to effective teaching.

Chapter 10

Corrective Teaching

Children are constantly testing limits. In many respects, this is healthy. Testing limits is one way they learn and grow and find out about the world around them. However, when kids continually test the limits set by parents, it can cause problems for the whole family.

The problem behaviors of children vary from one child to the next. For each of your children, what behaviors aggravate you the most? When do these behaviors take place? Where do these behaviors take place? How often do they take place? The more you specify the problem behaviors, the more likely you are to find a solution to them.

Corrective Teaching is our method of dealing with many of the problems parents face. In fact, many of them can't wait for us to present this section in our *Common Sense Parenting* classes. The following comments might tell you why parents feel that way:

- "I always have to ask two or three times whenever I want my kids to do something."

- "It seems like my kids argue all the time. And, about the dumbest things. They just pick, pick, pick at one another until one of them gets mad."

- "I can't get my kids to stop watching TV. They don't do their homework, they don't help out. They just want to watch TV."

- "I can't get them to help with the dishes unless I threaten to take away a privilege."

- "When I ask my son about his homework, he says it's done or he left it at school. Sooner or later, he gets a down slip from school."

- "It's to the point where I don't even look in my kid's rooms, let alone ask the kids to clean them. Those rooms are disaster areas."

- "My daughter leaves her toys all over the house. I just feel like selling all of them at a garage sale."

Well, you get the picture. One parent summed up the frustration many parents feel when she said, "What can I do? I've had it! I feel like all I do is yell all day. They think I'm an ogre but I can't get them to do a thing!"

This parent, like most concerned parents, was looking for a constructive, effective way to respond to her child's constant misbehavior.

We taught her a four-step process called Corrective Teaching.

What Is Corrective Teaching?

Corrective Teaching combines clear messages with consequences and practice to help parents respond to problem behavior. This is much like you have practiced in the previous chapters — just a little more detailed:

1. **Stop the problem behavior**

2. **Give a consequence.**

3. **Describe what you want.**

4. **Practice what you want.**

When to Use Corrective Teaching

Basically, you use Corrective Teaching anytime your kids do something they're not supposed to do. Simply, when they are:

1. Doing something you've asked them not to do;

2. Not doing something you've asked them to do;

3. Doing something that could result in harm to your kids or other people.

This includes things that are morally or legally wrong, or that are dangerous. In each of these situations, parents need to change what their children are doing.

Exercise 1

On the lines below, write down five of your child's common problem behaviors that you would like to change.

1. _____

_____

2. _____

_____

3. _____

_____

4. _____

_____

5. _____

_____

Here are some problem behaviors other parents put on their list:

1. My kids watch TV instead of doing homework.

2. My daughter complains about going to bed earlier than her older brothers.

3. My daughter brings the car home with the fuel gauge on "empty."

4. My teenage son leaves home without telling me where he's going.

5. My 4-year-old hits her little brother.

These are all situations when Corrective Teaching can be used. Now let's see how we can use the four steps to correct the problem.

Examples

Let's take a look at the four steps and some examples of how parents have used them to respond to their child's misbehavior.

In the first example, a parent had told his son to begin his homework. When the parent comes back in the room, his son is watching TV.

1. **Stop the problem behavior**

   • Calmly get their attention

   • Give a clear instruction

   • Describe what happened or is happening

   "Morris, please turn off the TV. I know you like to watch TV but you're supposed to be doing your homework."

2. **Give a consequence**

   • Relate it to the problem behavior

   "Since you were watching TV instead of doing your homework, leave the TV off for one hour after you finish your assignments."

3. **Describe what you want**

   • Be specific

   "When I ask you to get started on your homework, I want you to stop what you are doing and begin right away. If you can

do this, you can get back to what you were doing as soon as you are finished."

4. **Practice what you want**

   • Keep it brief

   • Praise during practice

   "Now here's a chance for you to show me you can do what we've talked about. You've done a good job listening so far. Now it's time for you to get your books and start studying."

In the second situation, a 5-year-old is pestering her father while he is on the telephone. The father has excused himself from the call and is sitting down to get at eye level with his daughter.

1. **Stop the problem behavior**

   • Calmly get their attention

   • Give a clear instruction

   • Describe what happened or is happening

   "Alice, please sit up here on the chair. While I was talking on the phone you kept repeating, 'Daddy, I want more peanut butter.'"

2. **Give a consequence**

   • Relate to problem behavior

   "Because you interrupted me while I was on the phone, I want you to sit on your chair for two minutes."

(With young children, parents report that they find it helpful to have the child sit on the chair, first. After the child sits for the required time, then they tell the child what to do in future situations. For a more detailed description of Time-Out and its use with younger children, see Appendix B.)

3. **Describe what you want**

   • Be specific

   "When you want something and I'm on the phone, please wait until I hang up. OK? Then I can hear what you say and give you an answer."

4. **Practice what you want**

   • Keep it brief

• Praise during practice

"Let's pretend that I'm on the phone. Look up and see me on the phone and then go back to playing until I hang it up . . . Alright! Good job of waiting. Thanks. Let's get that peanut butter now."

Exercise 2

In each of the blank spaces that follow, write down a situation involving one of your child's problem behaviors and how you would respond with each of the steps. Use your list of problem behaviors from earlier in this chapter as a prompt for getting started.

Situation _____

_____

1. **Stop the problem behavior:**

   _____

   _____

2. **Give a consequence:**

   _____

   _____

3. **Describe what you want:**

   _____

   _____

4. **Practice what you want:**

   _____

   _____

Exercise 2 (con't)

Situation _____

_____

1. Stop the problem behavior:

_____

_____

2. Give a consequence:

_____

_____

3. Describe what you want:

_____

_____

4. Practice what you want:

_____

_____

Situation _____

_____

1. Stop the problem behavior:

_____

_____

2. Give a consequence:

_____

_____

3. Describe what you want:

_____

_____

4. Practice what you want:

_____

_____

Now that you have given Corrective Teaching a try in writing, practice it in front of the mirror a few times before using it with one of your kids. Mirrors are a friendly place to start; they don't talk back as much as children. Once you've seen and heard yourself, and you feel like you're willing to give it a try with your child, go to it. Practice leads to confidence and confidence leads to success.

Using Corrective Teaching

Remain calm. Easy to say, but not always easy to do. Parents consistently tell us this is one of the most important pieces of the puzzle. Sometimes, kids misbehave so darn often that parents respond angrily. Or, the behavior itself is so annoying that parents react abruptly or nega-

tively. Please remember—stop, think about what you need to do, calm yourself, and proceed with Corrective Teaching. You are much more likely to effectively change your child's behavor when you do.

Stick to one issue. We don't know about your kids, but most kids are masters at getting us sidetracked. Some kids can get parents so far off the topic that they forget what the topic is. Familiar lines such as the following are particularly effective:

"You don't love me!"

"My friends don't have to do that. Their parents are nice."

"I don't want to talk about that. And, you can't make me."

"You can take away anything you want. I just don't care."

"I can't wait until I'm a parent. I'll do nice things for my kids."

Certainly, these types of comments go straight to a parent's heart. We've all wanted to tell our kids the myriad of nice things we do for them, or to prove what good parents we are. Don't try to justify your existence. Stick with what you want to teach. Let your kids know that if they really want to talk about other topics, they can bring them up after the main issue is resolved.

Give them a chance to earn something back. If your child is attentive and works to make up for the misbehavior, and you are pleased with the attempt, don't hesitate to give some part of the consequence back. For example, during Corrective Teaching, you took away one hour of TV time because your son and daughter were arguing. After you finished, both of the children apologized and said they would work together to clean the dishes. If they cooperate, you could give back 15 or 20 minutes of the TV time you took away. Doing this allows you to give them a positive consequence for working on the problem. This is an effective way to teach children to make up for mistakes or misbehaviors.

Be consistent. While the world around us is constantly changing, it helps to have some consistency in our lives. This means if the kids' bedtime is 9:30 each night, then they should be in bed on time. If they do, let them know it. Use Effective Praise and some creative rewards. If they are late to bed, use Corrective Teaching and eliminate the rewards. The more consistent we are, the more consistent our children are. We need to provide stability in our children's often hectic lives.

Be flexible. Just when we said to be consistent, we throw you a curve and talk about flexibility. What we mean is that you should consistently use Corrective Teaching, but you can vary the way you use it. No one knows your child better than you. If you think that she'll learn more if you put the consequence at the end, then give it a try. If it works, then keep using it that way. If it doesn't work, then try another way. Two points are important with this approach:

1. Learn and use the steps the way they're presented, then adapt them. They are presented this way for a reason; it works for most parents this way. Plus it's easier to adapt something after you know what you're adapting.

2. In order to know if your teaching is working, you have to develop some way of keeping track of how your child is behaving. This may be a diary of sorts, or a calendar with little notes that lets you know how each day went and what improvements your kids made.

It works. Parents who take the time to use each of the steps of Corrective Teaching are amazed at how easy it is and how it helps to change problem behaviors. Their attitude about parenting takes an about-face. They don't hesitate to correct their children's misbehavior and teach them a better way to behave. Parenting certainly is no less of a challenge, but now they're able to see constructive results. They take the opportunity to teach whenever possible; they use Corrective Teaching comfortably and confidently. Corrective Teaching will work for you, too.

Notes _____

_____
_____
_____
_____
_____
_____
_____
_____
_____
_____
_____
_____
_____
_____
_____

Chapter 11

Teaching Self-Control

"You're a complete idiot. I can't stand you!"

"Get outa my face, you asshole!"

"No way! I ain't gonna do it, and you can't make me!"

One of the more frustrating aspects of parenting is dealing with an angry, defiant child who simply refuses to do what you ask. The child may be yelling, hitting, arguing, throwing objects, or threatening you. Your child's behavior can make you feel powerless, emotionally drained, or just plain furious.

If you have ever felt like this, you're not alone. Many parents face these situations frequently. One thing is certain, however: kids must learn that negative, aggressive behavior is not acceptable. And, it can be harmful to them and others. The sooner kids learn to control their actions, the more they will benefit. Our method has helped parents teach their children a better way. We call it "Teaching Self-Control."

There are two key parts to Teaching Self-Control: **Getting your child calmed down** and **follow-up teaching**. We'll talk about each part in detail, but first let's take a brief look at what often happens when a child yells at the parent or refuses to do what was asked.

In these situations, a child is certainly not interested in, and in some cases, not capable of discussing the situation rationally. Generally, a great deal of talking by the parent does little to improve the situation. Often, the more the parent talks, the louder the child yells. The more the child yells, the louder the parent talks — until the

parent is yelling, too. These unpleasant actions continue until someone decides that this argument is too painful and drops out. It can be the parent, who walks out of the room in disgust and anger. Or, it can be the child, who stomps off to the bedroom and slams the door shut. In either case, the problem has gotten worse, not better.

If you've had to deal with a situation like this, you know how helpless a parent feels. Teaching Self-Control gives parents a way to respond that can help improve these situations.

We all get angry at times. But, when anger with another family member is vented through aggressive behavior, it becomes harmful to everyone involved. We want to teach our kids self-control so they can identify how they're feeling and learn how to deal with these behaviors in ways that won't lead to aggressive or harmful behavior.

What Is Teaching Self-Control?

The goal of Teaching Self-Control is to teach your children how to control their behavior when they get upset.

The first part of Teaching Self-Control is geared to helping you and your child become calm. This way, both the parent and child can work to resolve the disagreement. Very little can be accomplished if anger takes the place of logic.

The second part of Teaching Self-Control gives you an opportunity to teach your child some acceptable ways of behaving — some options — when your child is upset. Like the other skills you have learned, Teaching Self-Control emphasizes giving clear descriptions of your child's behaviors, using consequences, and teaching the behavior you want to see.

Let's take a look at the steps of Teaching Self-Control:

Part 1: Calming Down

1. Describe the problem behavior

- Describe what happened or is happening

- Clearly tell your child what he or she is doing wrong

2. Give clear instructions

- Describe what you want your child to do

- Give options for calming down

3. Allow time to calm down

- Make sure each person has time to regain control

- Decide what to teach next

Part 2: Follow-Up Teaching

4. Describe what your child could do differently next time

- Give your child other ways to handle the situation

5. Practice what your child can do next time

6. Give a consequence

Why Teach Self-Control?

Let's think about this for a minute.

If your 4-year-old throws himself on the floor and kicks and screams to get his way every time he gets frustrated or upset with someone or something, how do think he will try to get what he wants next time? Right. He will throw a tantrum.

If your 8-year-old argues and whines until you give in, what do you think will happen the next time she wants something? Exactly. She will whine.

If your teen yells and threatens you when you tell him he can't have the car this weekend, and he eventually gets to use it anyway, what do you think will happen the next time you tell him he can't use the car? Yes. Yelling and threatening.

So when we ask, "Why teach self-control?", the answer is clear. You want your child to be able to respond to frustrating situations in ways that will be helpful, not harmful. Maintaining self-control helps people get along with family members, do better in school, develop friendships, keep jobs, and have opportunities that would otherwise be lost. The list of benefits is limited only by the person who does not practice self-control.

When to Use Teaching Self-Control

Basically, parents report that they use Teaching Self-Control in two types of situations:

1. When their child misbehaves and will not respond to Corrective Teaching. Instead, the child continues or worsens the misbehavior.

2. When their child "blows up" — an emotional outburst that is sudden and intense, and the child refuses to do anything that the parents ask.

In either situation, the parents must teach their child self-control. Let's look at each step in Teaching Self-Control in more detail.

Part 1: Calming Down

1. Describe the problem behavior

Briefly tell your child exactly what he or she is doing wrong. We emphasize "briefly" here. Your child is not always interested in listening to what you have to say at this time, so saying a lot won't help. You will have time to describe the problem in detail once your child settles down. Remember to be clear and specific with what you do say. You should talk in a calm, level voice tone. Don't speak rapidly or try to say too much. For example, "Marcus, you're yelling at me and pacing around the room," gives the child a clear message about what he is doing.

Often, parents say judgmental things when they dislike their child's behavior. They say things such as, "Quit acting like a baby," or "You have a lousy attitude." We suggest that you simply describe what your child is doing wrong without becoming angry or accusatory.

It also is helpful to use empathy. As we said earlier, empathy means that you show understanding for the other person's feelings. For instance, you might say "I know you are upset right now. And, I know what happened made you unhappy." This starts the teaching sequence positively and shows your child that you care. Plus, it often helps you focus on your child's behavior rather than your own emotions.

Exercise 2

Think back to the situation you described before. What specific behaviors could you have described to your child? Write those on the lines provided: _____

_____

_____

_____

_____

Are you satisfied that your descriptions are clear and specific? Are they brief? Could you have used an empathy statement? Did you use words that your child could easily understand?

2. Give clear instructions

Tell your child exactly what you want him or her to do. Your purpose here is to help your child regain self-control. Simple instructions like, "Please come over here and sit down," or "Please stop yelling at me," clearly state what your child needs to do. Don't give too many instructions or repeat them constantly, or you will appear to lecture or badger your child. Simple, clear instructions keep the focus on having your child regain self-control.

Make calming statements to your child like, "Take a few deep breaths and try to settle down." As when describing the problem behavior, keep your words to a minimum.

Notes _____

_____

_____

_____

_____

_____

Exercise 3

Take the behaviors you described in Part 1, and write down instructions you could have given to your child.

_____

_____

_____

_____

It is very important that parents practice these first two steps. The emphasis is on using clear messages to help calm your child. Practicing this skill is time worth investing. Besides giving your child important information about his or her behavior, clear messages help keep you on track.

3. Allow time to calm down

Parents tell us that this is the most important step in the whole process. If parents remain calm, it increases the likelihood that their child will calm down faster. Parents also tell us that remembering this step has helped them focus on their child's behavior. Simply saying, "We both need a little time to calm down. I'll be back in a few minutes," can be very effective. Remember, sometimes giving your child a little "space" helps your child "save face."

As parents take the time to calm down, they can think of what they are going to teach next. This also allows the child to make a decision—to continue misbehaving or to calm down.

Come back as often as necessary. Ask questions like, "Can we talk about what happened?" or "Are you calmed down enough to talk to me?"

Move to the next phase when your child is able to answer you in a reasonably calm voice and will pay attention to what you say. You're not going to have the happiest child at this point, but it's important that he or she can talk without losing self-control again.

Take your time. Give descriptions and instructions as needed. Most of all, be calm and in control of your emotions.

Part 2: Follow-up Teaching

4. Describe what your child can do differently next time

Give your child another way to express frustration or anger. Kids have to learn that when they "blow up" every time something doesn't go their way, it leads to more negative consequences.

We teach many of our parents to rely on the "Instead of . . ." phrase. It goes like this: "Instead of yelling and running out the door, just look at me and say 'OK.'" "Instead of cussing, why don't you take a deep breath and think of how to answer me." "Instead of pacing the floor, why don't you sit on the couch?"

The purpose of this phrase is to get kids to _think_. The next time they're in a negative situation, if they just think about what happened, possibly something will click, and they will remember not to make the situation worse.

Exercise 4

Take the example you used in Part 1, and write down what you could tell your child to do differently next time:

_____

_____

_____

_____

5. Practice

Now that your child knows what to do, it's important that he or she knows how to do it. By practicing, you are more likely to see the behavior you want the next time your child starts to get upset.

After the practice is over, let your child know what was done correctly and what needs improvement. Be as positive as you can be, especially if your child is making a concerted effort to do what you ask.

6. Give a consequence

This is a crucial part of Teaching Self-Control. If there is a common mistake made by the parents we work with, it is that they forget to give a consequence. They got too wrapped up in stopping their child's negative behavior. Or, they were so pleased once all the yelling stopped that giving a consequence didn't cross their minds. Others told us that they just didn't have the heart to give a consequence because they didn't want to upset their child any more than he already was. Consequences help change behavior; use them.

We emphasize that you consistently apply a negative consequence each time your child loses self-control. And, stick with whatever consequence you give. Sometimes, after the situation is all over, parents want to ease up, or their children convince them to forget it all together. If you have given an appropriate negative consequence, follow through with it. Over time, angry outbursts will diminish and your child will learn self-control.

Exercise 5

In your example, list a consequence you would give:

_____

_____

_____

_____

Let's take a look at a quick example of Teaching Self-Control. Here's the situation: You have just told your 10-year-old son that he can't go over to his friend's house because he hasn't finished cleaning his room. He yells, "You idiot! I hate you! You never let me do anything!" Then, he runs to his room screaming and cussing.

Part l: Calming Down

1. Describe the problem behavior

- Describe what happened or is happening

- Clearly tell the child what he is doing wrong

  "I know you wanted to go to your friend's house, but you are yelling and swearing."

2. Give clear instructions

- Describe what you want him to do

- Give options for calming down

  "Why don't you stop yelling and sit in your room and calm down."

3. Allow time to calm down

- Give everyone a chance to calm themselves

  (Leave the area for a few minutes. Come back and ask if he is willing to talk.)

- Check for cooperative behavior

  "Can we talk about this now?" or "I can see that you're still upset. I'll be back in a few minutes."

When your child is following directions and is willing to talk with you about the problem, you move from the calming down phase to follow-up teaching.

Part 2: Follow-Up Teaching

4. Describe what your child can do differently next time

- Think of a better way your child can react when he gets upset

  "Ralph, let's look at what you can do the next time you get upset. What I'd like you to do is ask me if you can go to your room and calm down."

5. Practice what your child can do next time

- Increase the chance that your child will do what you've talked about

  "Why don't you give that a try? I'm going to tell you that you can't go out and play. What should you do? ... Right. OK, let's try it."

- Let him know how he practiced

  "Great! You asked me if you could go to your room. And, you asked me in a nice voice tone. Thanks a lot."

6. Give a consequence

- Help prevent the problem from occurring again

  "Remember, we have a consequence for yelling and swearing. Tonight, you'll have to do the dishes and sweep the floor after dinner."

Remember, this is an example. In real-life situations, your child probably won't cooperate this quickly. He or she may go from being out of control to being calm, and then suddenly being out of control again. Some kids have a lot of stamina when they're upset. There also may be other distractions you will have to deal with in these situations; for example, your other kids need something, the phone rings, the soup is boiling over on the stove, and so on. Interactions with your child do not occur in a vacuum. Continue teaching. In these instances, use the skills you learned in the "Staying Calm" chapter, and adapt the teaching steps and your teaching style to the situation. Stick to simple descriptions and instructions, continue to use empathy, and stay calm.

Skills Taught in Follow-Up Teaching

Here are some skills that parents frequently find helpful to teach during Follow-Up Teaching:

- How to stay calm
- How to ask for help
- How to accept criticism
- How to accept "No" for an answer
- How to follow instructions
- How to disagree with others

Most often, these skills help children handle stressful situations in constructive ways. See Appendix D for detailed descriptions of these skills.

Helpful Hints

Staying calm. Staying calm is much easier when you stay on task. Implement all of the steps of Teaching Self-Control. Concentrating on your child's behavior is much easier when you have a framework to follow. Teaching Self-Control gives you a set of effective steps for responding to your children when you need it most. Those are the times when you are the most frustrated, upset, or exasperated. Your children may try to argue with what you say or call you names. They may say you don't love them or tell you how unfair you are. They may say things to make you feel guilty or angry or useless. If you get caught up in all of these side issues, you lose sight of your original purpose—to teach your child self-control. And, you can lose sight of the original problem and how you need to deal with it. If you find yourself responding to what your child is saying, remember to use a key phrase — "We'll talk about that when you calm down." Staying on task ensures that you won't start arguing or losing your temper.

Physical actions. Throughout the process be aware of your physical actions. Some parents find that sitting helps calm the situation quickly. When they stand up—particularly fathers—they tend to be more threatening. This only makes matters worse and lessens the likelihood that the child will calm himself.

Pointing your index finger, hands on your hips, scowling, leaning over your child, and raising a fist are all examples of physical actions that tend to increase tension in these emotionally charged situations. Try your best to avoid these gestures. Keep your hands in your pockets, cross them over your chest—find something to do with them other than waving them at your child.

Planned consequences. It helps to have consequences set up in advance. For example, "Sarah, when I tell you 'No,' sometimes you want to argue with me. Then you get real mad and start yelling. From now on, if you do this, you will lose your phone privileges for two nights." Then explain to Sarah why she needs to accept decisions and why she shouldn't argue or scream. Planned consequences are consistent; if Sarah loses self-control, she is aware of what negative consequence she will receive. Also, planned consequences help avoid giving unreasonable or harsh consequences that stem from your anger.

The completion of Teaching Self-Control. As your child calms down and you complete the teaching sequence, there can be numerous side issues that arise. For example, some situations may call for a problem-solving approach. Your child possibly doesn't have the knowledge or experience to deal with a certain situation. Take the time to help find solutions.

Other situations may call for a firm, matter-of-fact ending to Teaching Self-Control. "OK, we've practiced what to do. Now, go in your brother's room and pleasantly apologize to him."

Still other situations may call for an empathic, understanding approach. Some kids cry after an intense situation. They just don't know how to handle what they're feeling inside. "Let's sit down and talk about why you've been feeling so angry. Maybe I can help. At least, I can listen."

Take the opportunity to help your child by whatever you feel is the best approach. Sometimes, going through the rough times together form the tightest emotional bonds.

Parents must have a bountiful supply of patience if their kids have a problem with self-control. The wisest parents are those who realize that learning self-control is an ongoing process. We are skeptical—as you should be—of anyone who claims that self-control can be taught immediately. We know it takes a long time. Don't try to rush the learning process; expecting too much too soon can create more problems than it solves. Be attentive to small accomplishments; praise even the smallest bit of progress your child makes. (And, while you're at it, give yourself a big pat on the back. Teaching self-control is a tough job, and you wouldn't do it if you didn't love your child.)

As you teach self-control, look for positive changes; your child possibly will have fewer angry outbursts, or the outbursts won't last as long, or they won't have nearly the intensity they once had.

Teaching Self-Control helps parents and children break the painful argument cycle. When tension is greatest in the family, Teaching Self-Control gives everyone a constructive way to get problems resolved.

Notes _____
_____
_____
_____
_____
_____
_____
_____
_____
_____
_____
_____
_____
_____
_____
_____
_____
_____
_____
_____
_____
_____
_____
_____

Encouraging Communication in Families

Chapter 12

Making Decisions

No matter what their age, kids are making decisions all the time.

> *A 4-year-old watches his ball roll out into the street. What does he do?*

> *A 10-year-old is asked by a friend to copy her homework. What does she do?*

> *A 16-year-old is offered some beer at a party. What does he do?*

In each situation, these kids have to make a decision. Kids frequently make decisions on the spur of the moment, sometimes without thinking. They tend to look at solutions to problems as black or white, all or nothing, yes or no, do it or don't do it. Kids also focus on the situation at hand and have difficulty looking ahead to see how a decision could affect them later.

So, how can parents prepare their children to make the best decisions?

The SODAS Method

At Boys Town, we use a five-step problem-solving method called SODAS. The principles are simple, yet this method is adaptable to many situations. The SODAS method accomplishes two goals.

First, it gives parents and children a process for solving problems and making decisions together.

Second, it helps parents teach children how to solve problems and make decisions on their own.

The SODAS method helps both children and adults think more clearly and make a decision based on sound reasoning.

SODAS stands for:

1. Situation

2. Options

3. Disadvantages

4. Advantages

5. Solution

Let's look at each step of the SODAS process.

Define the Situation

Before you can solve a problem, you need to know what the problem is. Defining the situation sometimes takes the greatest amount of time because children often use vague or emotional descriptions. Also, kids aren't always aware that a certain situation could cause problems. A 4-year-old may think that running into the street isn't a problem; he's only thinking about getting his ball back. He doesn't realize the dangers of his actions.

Other decisions may not contain obvious dangers, but they still may contain drawbacks. Regardless, these are opportunities for your child to make a choice. Kids will have to decide how to spend their allowance, what kids to hang around with, or whether to go out for sports or get a job. Kids can quickly run through the SODAS process to make these daily decisions.

Tips for defining the **Situation:**

1. **Ask specific, open-ended questions to determine the situation.** Avoid asking questions that your child can answer with a one-word answer; "Yes," "No," "Fine," "Good," etc. Instead, ask questions such as, "What did you do then?" or "What happened after you said that?" These questions help you piece together what occurred.

2. **Teach children to focus on the entire situation, not just part of it.** For example, questions that identify who, what, when and where help you get a clear picture of the whole situation.

3 **Summarize the information.** Sometimes, kids get so overwhelmed by the emotions surrounding a problem that they lose sight of what the actual problem is. State the problem in the simplest, most specific form. Ask your child if your summary of the situation is correct.

Options

Once you have a complete description of the situation, you can begin discussing options— the choices your child has. There usually are several options to each problem.

Kids, however, frequently think of solutions in the form of "all or nothing" options. For example, a student gets a bad grade on a test and immediately wants to change classes since everything is "ruined." It's common for kids to only see one solution to a problem, or take the first one that pops into their heads. Other times, they may see no options at all.

Your role as a parent is to get your child to think. Ask questions like, "Can you think of anything else you could do?" or "What else could solve the problem?" Consistently asking these questions helps your child learn a process to use when making decisions without your guidance.

Exercise 1

Describe a current situation where your child needs to make a decision. It could concern school, friends, playtime, or any other area of your child's life. As we discuss each step of the SODAS method, we will ask you to use this situation through the whole process.

Situation _____

_____

_____

_____

_____

_____

Tips for identifying **Options:**

1. **Let your child list good and bad options.** Don't give approval or disapproval at this time. It's a common tendency for parents to cut right to the quick and tell their kids what they think. But, the purpose here is to get your child to think of ways to make a decision on his or her own.

2. **Limit the options to four or less.** Any more than that tends to get confusing. (Also, make sure at least one of the options has a chance for success.)

3. **Suggest options if your child is having trouble coming up with them.** This way, kids learn that in many situations there is more than one option.

Exercise 2

Using the situation you described earlier, identify 3 or 4 possible options for resolving the problem. Jot down what your child would pick, as well as options you might pick. Write them on the lines below.

Options

1. _____

_____

2. _____

_____

3. _____

_____

4. _____

_____

Discuss Disadvantages/Advantages

In this step, you help your child look at the pros and cons of each option. This helps your child see the connection between each option and what could happen if that option is chosen.

Tips for reviewing **Disadvantages** and **Advantages**:

1. **Ask your child for his or her thoughts about each option**. What's good about the option? What's bad about the option? Why would the option work? Why wouldn't the option work?

2. **Help your child come up with both disadvantages and advantages for every option**. This will be easier for your child to do with certain options; he or she may not have the experience or knowledge to know possible outcomes for all options.

Exercise 3

List possible disadvantages and advantages for each option that you listed on the last exercise.

Disadvantages

1. _____

_____

2. _____

_____

3. _____

_____

4. _____

_____

Advantages

1. _____

_____

2. _____

_____

3. _____

_____

4. _____

_____

Choosing a Solution

At this point it is time to find which option would work best. Quickly summarize the disadvantages and advantages to each option and ask your child to choose the best one.

Tips for choosing a **Solution**:

1. **Make sure that your child knows the options and the possible outcomes of each one.** You're trying to help your child make an informed decision and establish a pattern for making future decisions.

2. **Some decisions are hard to make.** If the decision doesn't need to be made immediately, let your child take some time for additional thought.

Exercise 4

List the best possible solution (option) to the problem you described in the previous exercises.

Solution _____

_____

_____

_____

_____

Final Thoughts

Parents usually have a lot of questions about SODAS and the types of situations in which it can be used. Here are are some things to think about when using the SODAS method.

Sometimes kids pick options that don't sit too well with their parents. In general, if the decisions won't hurt anyone, isn't illegal or contrary to your moral or religious beliefs, then let them make the choice and learn from their decision. For example, your son might insist that he wants to spend most of his money on a very expensive video game. You may not agree with his choice but it won't harm anyone if he decides to buy the game. Let him buy it and learn from the consequences. Perhaps he will enjoy the game so much he won't mind not having money for other activities. Or he might wish later that he had not bought such an expensive game. Either way he'll learn from his decision.

Occasionally, kids face options that are illegal, immoral or that will cause harm to themselves or others. In these cases, parents have found it helpful to clearly state their disapproval, reiterate the disadvantages to that solution, and let their child know the consequences of making that choice. For example, if your 16-year-old daughter decides that she wants to drink when out with her friends, you can let her know that you don't want her to be drinking and spell out all of the many dangers. Parents can state what consequences they will give her if she decides to drink. But, sometimes, despite all of our efforts, kids still make wrong decisions. When that occurs, it is necessary to follow through with the consequences you described. Then, help your child go back through the SODAS process and come up with more acceptable solutions.

While we want to encourage kids to make decisions on their own, we need to let them know that we'll be there to help at any time. This includes supporting them as they implement the solution. If the solution does not work out the way the child planned, you will be there to offer support and empathy. You and your child can then return to the SODAS format to find another solution to the problem.

Practice putting the solution in effect. The best you can do is help your child reach a reasonable solution and practice implementing it. The purpose of practice is to help your child feel confident about what solution has been chosen.

Check with your child to see how the solution worked. Set a specific time to talk about this. This is an excellent opportunity for you to praise your child on following through with the decision. You also can look for additional solutions, if necessary.

In Exercise 5, we have used the first four steps of SODAS. Which option would you choose if the child in the example were your child?

Exercise 5

Situation

Ten-year-old Billy comes home from school and tells you that another kid slapped him. As you ask questions, you find out that Billy was telling jokes, and the other kid overheard and thought Billy was making fun of him. The kid came over and said, "Quit laughing at me," and slapped him, then quickly walked away.

Options	Disadvantages	Advantages
1. Tell the teacher.	Other kid would think I'm a snitch.	Kid might not do it again.
2. Talk to other kid and explain.	Don't know the kid that well. He might think I'm lying.	He might believe me and apologize.
3. Forget it.	He'll still think I called him names.	It may never happen again.
4. Have my parents call his parents.	Then a lot of adults get involved and things might get more complicated.	His parents could explain the whole story to him.

Solution

Which option do you think your child would pick? _____

_____

_____

Which option would you pick? _____

_____

_____

This is just one of many possible situations where kids need to learn how to solve problems. SODAS is an excellent process for teaching your child how to make decisions. It is practical and can be applied in many different situations that your child will face. You can feel confident that you have given your child an effective, easy-to-use method for solving problems.

Chapter 13

Reaching Goals With Charts and Contracts

Is there ever a situation in a family when parents and kids both get what they want? You bet there is. In *Common Sense Parenting*, we use a successful approach that uses charts and contracts. These methods assist parents in helping their kids set and reach reasonable goals.

A contract is a written statement of:

1. What your child agrees to do.

2. What the consequences are if he or she accomplishes that goal.

A chart is a contract that uses pictures to illustrate and keep track of an agreement between you and your child.

Example

Parents' Goals for Their Children

1. Keep bedroom clean

2. Do homework

3. Take out the trash

4. Come home on time

Children's Goals for Themselves

1. Have friends over

2. Stay out later

3. Earn more allowance

4. Use the car

Charts and contracts involve parents making certain things available when their children do certain other things. If this sounds familiar, it is. Charts and contracts are a written form of Grandma's Rule.

Using the lists above, parents allow their son to have friends over when he keeps his room clean for a week. Another parent might allow his daughter to stay out later when she does her homework consistently. And so on.

Before kids get to do what they want, they have to keep their end of the bargain. Charts and contracts are simple, straightforward, and geared toward helping parents and children make improvements and get things accomplished. Other important benefits to helping children set and reach goals with charts or contracts include:

- **More opportunity for success** — Charts and contracts help us spell out what we expect from our kids. Children are more likely to be able to reach a goal when they know exactly what to do.

- **Improved self-esteem** — Charts and contracts can help children be more successful. When successful, children generally feel better about themselves.

- **Improved communication between parent and child** — Identifying goals and planning together requires conversation between parent and child. For both to be winners, negotiation is necessary. The time spent setting up charts or contracts shows your children you care and are interested in helping them succeed.

When Do You Use Charts and Contracts?

For the ongoing day-to-day problems that kids present, you'll want to use Corrective Teaching or Teaching Self-Control. Charts and contracts can be used when:

1. **You want to focus on a particular problem behavior.** For example, inconsistently completing homework, frequently complaining or whining when asked to do something, having tantrums, or always running late for school in the morning are typical behaviors parents target.

2. **Your child has a goal she'd like to achieve.** For example, making the baseball team, earning money for a new bike, getting better grades, or being able to stay out later on weekends are common goals children set for themselves.

3. **You have a particular goal you'd like your child to achieve.** For example, starting and adding to a savings account, getting involved in school activities, mowing the lawn, or getting a job are common goals parents set for their children.

Getting Started

Let's take a look at how you can use charts or contracts.

Exercise 1

In the spaces below, make a short list of things you'd like your child to do.

1._____

_____

2._____

_____

3._____

_____

Good. Now, list three things your child would like to do. (Within reason, of course. Sailing to Tahiti is probably not an option.) If you have any difficulty here, think back to the last three times your child asked you to do something. Better yet, ask your child to help you with the list.

Exercise 2

List three things your child would like to do.

1._____

_____

2._____

_____

3._____

_____

Here are some examples of things other parents have wanted their children to do.

1. Go to bed on time without a big fuss.

2. Finish their homework each night.

3. Ask permission before they make plans.

4. Bring the car home on time.

5. Come home at curfew.

6. Get to school on time each day.

7. Get themselves ready for school each morning without having to be reminded.

8. Do their chores around the house.

9. Offer to help out.

10. Keep their room clean.

Here are some of the things kids have put on their list of things to do.

1. Have more allowance.

2. Have a later curfew.

3. Stay overnight at a friend's house.

4. Use the car on the weekends.

5. Get to go more places.

6. Not have to do so many chores around the house.

7. Buy new clothes.

8. Stay up later.

9. Have more play time with their parents.

10. Pick a movie to rent.

These two lists are samples of what parents want for their children and what children want for themselves. Now let's see how you can combine the two lists and put a contract together.

Writing Contracts

Of course, these contracts are not formal, legal documents. A contract may be nothing more than a piece of note paper, written in pencil and stuck to the refrigerator. But, it is an agreement reached by you and your child. Here are the steps for writing effective contracts.

1. Identify goals — yours and your child's.

2. Write what you want your child to do.

3. Write what your child wants to do.

4. Set a time limit.

5. Date and sign the contract.

Examples

Here's how this might work with a 15-year-old girl who wants a later curfew and her parents who want her to come home on time.

1. Identify goals — yours and your child's.

- *Parent's goal*: Parent wants child to be more responsible and come home on time.

- *Child's goal:* Child wants more freedom and a later curfew.

2. Write what you want your child to do.

- Be home by 9:00 p.m. Sunday through Thursday and 10:00 p.m. on Friday and Saturday for two weeks in a row.

3. Write what your child wants to do.

- Move curfew back to 10:30 p.m. on Friday and Saturday nights.

4. Set a time limit.

- Pick a specific time each evening when you and your child review progress. This continues for two weeks or until the contract is renegotiated.

5. Date and sign the contract.

- Signatures indicate that the contract is in effect. Signatures also indicate that you and your child feel this is a fair agreement.

Examples
Shawna's Curfew Agreement

I, Shawna, agree to be home by 9 o'clock on Sunday through Thursday nights and by 10 o'clock on Friday and Saturday nights. I have to do this for two weeks in a row before I get a later weekend curfew. If I am late coming home, I lose going out the following night. My two weeks of coming home on time begin again the next time I go out.

We, Mom and Dad, agree to let Shawna stay out until 10:30 p.m. on Friday and Saturday nights when she comes home on time for two weeks in a row.

We will mark the calendar each night after Shawna comes home on time. This will continue for two weeks or until the contract is renegotiated.

_____

(Shawna's signature)   (Date)

_____

(Parents' signature)

Here's another example of a contract. In this situation, the parent and child discussed completing homework consistently in exchange for watching TV.

Ronnie's Read and Watch Agreement

I, Ronnie, will study for at least 30 minutes every evening (Sunday through Thursday) before asking to watch TV. I will start my homework assignments at 5 o'clock each day. If they take longer than 30 minutes, I will work on them until they're finished. I understand that if I don't do my homework, I don't get to watch TV.

I, Ronnie's mom, will let Ronnie watch TV for one hour each night when he completes his homework as expected.

We will go over Ronnie's homework each night when he is finished. We will continue this contract for two weeks.

_____
(Ronnie's signature)   (Date)

_____
(Mom's signature)

Developing Charts

Charts make it easy for kids to see their progress. Charts are very helpful with younger children who benefit from visual, concrete examples. They're also helpful with older kids, however.

Here are the steps for developing a chart.

1. Identify goals — yours and your child's.

2. Set a time limit.

3. Draw the chart.

Examples

Let's take a look at how this worked for Billy, 10, and his parents. Billy was interested in having later bedtimes, especially on weekends. Billy's parents wanted him to go to bed on time without arguing each night. They used the chart called "Billy's Bedtime Bonanza," shown on page 75, to help Billy go to bed on time.

Billy's bedtime on weeknights was 9 o'clock. Each weeknight that Billy went to bed on time

without arguing he put a star on the corresponding stair. (It can be a stick figure, happy face, or whatever symbol your child likes to use.) The number of times Billy reached the goal determined how late he got to stay up on Friday and Saturday. The more nights he went to bed on time, the later he got to stay up on the weekend. So, going to bed on time without arguing on three of the five weeknights earned a 9:45 p.m. bedtime on Friday and Saturday. There was an incentive built in for getting to bed every night on time. He increased his weekend bedtime by yet another half hour by getting that fifth night.

While this was set up to help Billy get to bed on time, the same idea can be used for several different goals, such as, homework completion, being ready for school on time in the morning, helping others each day, keeping the bedroom clean, and so on. Any of these goals could use a similar chart to get the job done.

At the end of this chapter are several examples of charts that can be adapted for your children. Many parents enjoy coming up with creative charts for their kids. Some of the most creative designs have come from the kids, themselves. Young children, in particular, love to get out the crayons and make a colorful chart. This is a positive way to get your child involved in the process and gives you one more thing to praise.

Hints for Successful Charts and Contracts

1. **State the goal positively.** Use "When you finish your homework, you can watch TV" instead of, "If you don't finish your homework, you don't get to watch TV." Either one of these can be true, but it's easier to reach a goal if you're working toward something positive.

2. **Follow through on the agreement.** Be sure to review your child's progress each day and provide encouragement to keep going. When your child reaches the goal, give what you promised. And, pile on the praise!

3. **Make the goals specific and measurable.** A goal of "completing homework each night" is easier to measure than "doing better in school." Likewise, it's easier to

BILLY'S BEDTIME BONANZA

**Weekday Bedtime
is 9:00 p.m.**

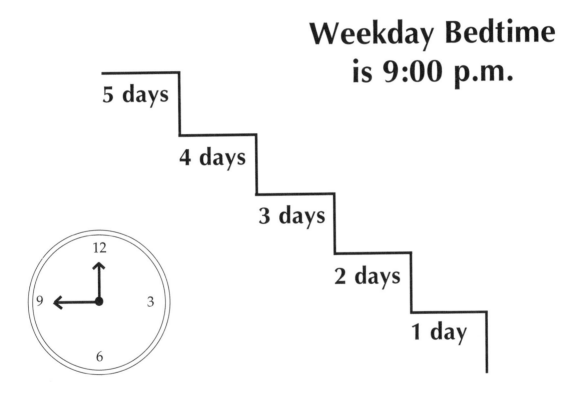

5 days

4 days

3 days

2 days

1 day

**Friday and Saturday
Bedtimes**

}

1 day = 9:15 p.m.
2 days = 9:30 p.m.
3 days = 9:45 p.m.
4 days = 10:00 p.m.
5 days = 10:30 p.m.

tell if your child is "offering to help Mom once a day" than "being more responsible." Being specific and clear lets you know when your child has reached the goal.

4. **Keep the goals reasonable.** Setting reachable goals is especially important when you are first introducing the idea of a chart or contract.

5. **Provide the consequence.** "What the parent agrees to do" is the positive consequence for your child. When the goal is reached, the consequence is given. If the goal isn't reached, the consequence isn't given. Remember Grandma's Rule.

6. **Make it fun**. Again, charts and contracts are used to help kids reach goals and experience success. This will be more enjoyable if it's fun for you and your child. Make a big deal out of each day's progress and use lots of praise during the day when your child is working toward the goal.

Charts and contracts are a great way to help children see that they can achieve success. Charts and contracts open lines of communication so parents and children achieve goals together.

The following charts are samples of how parents have combined a goal for their children with positive consequences. (Use the list of consequences you developed for your child in Chapter 3.) We've included a blank sample of each chart for you to photocopy for your own use.

Notes _____

_____

_____

_____

_____

_____

_____

_____

_____

_____

_____

_____

_____

_____

_____

_____

_____

_____

_____

_____

_____

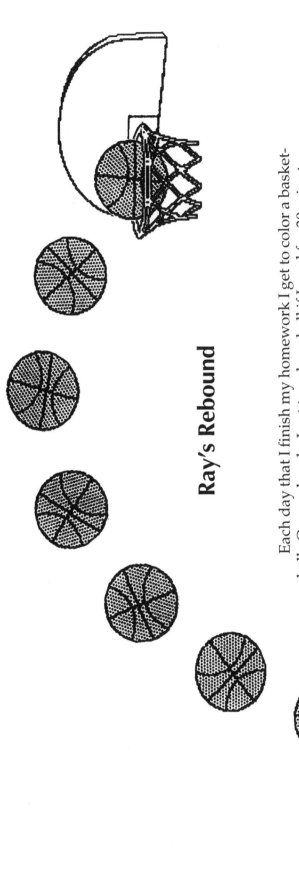

Ray's Rebound

Each day that I finish my homework I get to color a basketball. On weekends, I get to color a ball if I read for 30 minutes. Each day that I color a ball I get to shoot baskets outside with Mom for 15 minutes.

End of the Week Bonus

On Saturday, we'll count the number of times I finished my homework or read during the week. I get a bonus for having 4 or more balls colored each week.

4 balls colored = grocery shopping on Saturday

5 balls colored = friend comes over on Saturday afternoon

6 balls colored = bike ride on Sunday morning with dad

7 balls colored = friend stays overnight on Saturday

Megan's Morning

	Monday	Tuesday	Wednesday	Thursday	Friday	Saturday	Sunday
Get Dressed	★	★	★	★	★	★	★
Make Bed	★	★			★	★	
Eat Breakfast	★	★	★	★	★	★	★
Brush Teeth	★	★		★	★	★	
Ready for School on Time	★		★	★	★	★	★

Each day that I have **3 stars** I get to pick one of the following:
1. Call 1 friend on the phone
2. Ride my bike
3. Have the special glass at dinner

Each day that I have **4 stars** I get to pick two things to do. They can be from this list or the 3 star list.
1. Have a 15 minute later bedtime
2. Call 2 friends on the phone
3. Play a card game with mom or dad

Each day that I have **5 stars** I get to pick three things to do. They can be from any of the lists.
1. Have a 30 minute later bedtime
2. Have a friend over to play
3. Go to a friend's house to play

81

	Monday	Tuesday	Wednesday	Thursday	Friday	Saturday	Sunday
Get Dressed							
Make Bed							
Eat Breakfast							
Brush Teeth							
Ready for School on Time							

83

Cathy's On Time Calendar

I can get 4 happy faces each day. The number of happy faces tells me what special things I get to do each day.

1 **Happy Face** = Piggyback ride to bed
2 **Happy Faces** = Ride bike plus above
3 **Happy Faces** = Checkers before bed plus above
4 **Happy Faces** = 15 minute later bedtime plus above

	Sunday	Monday	Tuesday	Wednesday	Thursday	Friday	Saturday
☀	Up on time ☺	Up on time ☺	Up on time ☺	Up on time ☺	Up on time ☺	Late getting up	Up on time ☺
	Ready for Church ☺	Ready for school ☺	Late for school	Ready for school ☺	Ready for school ☺	Late for school	Ready for shopping ☺
⛅	Come in from play on time ☺	Home from school on time ☺	Home from school on time ☺	Late from school	Late from school	Home on time ☺	Come in from play on time ☺
☆☾	Late to bed	Bed on time ☺	Bed on time ☺	Bed on time ☺	Late to bed	Bed on time ☺	Bed on time ☺

85

On Time
_____ Calendar

I can get 4 happy faces each day. The number of happy faces tells me what special things I get to do each day.

1 Happy Face =
2 Happy Faces =
3 Happy Faces =
4 Happy Faces =

	Sunday	Monday	Tuesday	Wednesday	Thursday	Friday	Saturday
☀							
⛅							
☾★							

Sammy's "S" Curve

Behavior: <u>Playing nicely with your sister</u>

Reward <u>Mom reads a book to me.</u>

This is an "S" curve because "S" is the first initial of Sammy's name. You can use any letter or any number of circles to make your design. Each time Sammy's Mom found him playing nicely with his sister, he got to color in one of the circles. When he colored 3 circles he got the reward. This chart was set up to use one sheet each day.

Reward <u>Play catch for 15 minutes with Mom.</u>

Reward <u>Pick a snack.</u>

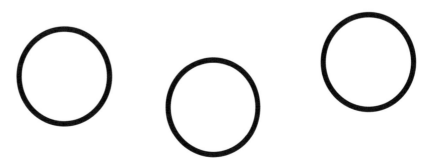

Name: _____

Behavior: _____

Reward _____

Reward _____

Reward _____

Chapter 14

Family Meetings

Today's families are busy. It's hard to spend time together. There is only so much time in a day and work, school, sports, organizations, and other activities greatly reduce the time for the family. One valuable tool we use at Boys Town is the Family Meeting.

Family Meeting is a time when all family members get together to share information and make decisions.

Exercise 1

What are some upcoming events that you and your kids can discuss?

1. _____

_____

2. _____

_____

3. _____

_____

4. _____

_____

Share Information

Schedules — Family Meeting is a great time to coordinate everyone's schedules. Your kids can tell you what upcoming activities they have; they can plan for school or for playing with friends. You can ask important questions like who needs supplies, transportation, money, or materials for the week. A home operates better when information like this is shared. It certainly makes life easier for mom and dad when plans are made in advance.

Praise — What an ideal time to praise each of your kids! And, to let everyone know what achievements or accomplishments have been made. Show your approval for improvements at school, for offers to help out around the house, or for getting along with another child. Let everyone know about attempts to solve problems. Don't wait for monumental achievements; it's the little things that make the big differences. And, think of creative ways for your kids to learn to praise one another. One family we know starts each meeting by having everyone say something nice about the person sitting to the right. This is a nice way to get the meeting started on a positive note.

Really important things — Here's a time for you and your kids to share information about all those other "things" going on in your lives. Give your kids a chance to talk about what happened in their school, what they discussed in class about local or world events, problems they're having with friends, and things they'd like to do

Exercise 2

What are some things your kids have done that you can share at Family Meeting?

1. _____

_____

2. _____

_____

3. _____

_____

4. _____

_____

Exercise 3

What are some things you'd like your kids to discuss with you — or you'd like to discuss with them?

1. _____

_____

2. _____

_____

3. _____

_____

4. _____

_____

as a family. You, too, get to share your opinion about these important issues. Be sure to bring some of your own "things" to discuss, like what you've been doing at work, current events, how local changes may impact you or your family, and your opinions of the latest fads or music. Family Meeting is a time to talk and listen, to share and discuss. This opportunity helps children develop their own views and beliefs by listening to the opinions of others. It can be fun, entertaining, and educational as it brings the family closer together.

Decisions Within Limits

Family Meeting is a nice place to have your kids share in making routine decisions. Decide what next week's menus should be, where to go on a family outing, which TV show to watch, or how household chores should be split up. Kids will be much happier if they have a chance to give their input when decisions are made. You'll be much happier if you set limits to what they

can decide. For example, your family wants to go to a movie as a family outing this weekend. You could say, "Kids, the first thing you need to decide is what night we should go out. Then, pick a 'P' or 'PG' movie that all of us will like." This way you let your children make decisions within limits you set. Your children get the choice of what night to go out and what movie to see. However, they do not get the choice of selecting an 'R' movie. That is a limit set by you.

By setting limits beforehand, you allow your kids the opportunity to learn how to make decisions (use the SODAS method) and be comfortable with the decisions they make.

Setting limits allows your kids safe parameters when making decisions. There are certain decisions you are not going to allow them to make, even if you ask for their input. Children do not have the experience or maturity that you do and they shouldn't be given responsibilities they can't handle. Major decisions, or decisions of a moral or legal nature should be decided by you.

Exercise 4

What are some routine decisions your kids can help
you make this week? What limits would you set?

Decision	Limits
1. _____	1. _____
_____	_____
2. _____	2. _____
_____	_____
3. _____	3. _____
_____	_____

Tips for Having Effective Family Meetings

1. **Keep Family Meeting short, no longer than 10-15 minutes**. Keep your topics simple enough to be solved easily. As your kids increase their skills, move ahead accordingly. In the beginning, however, your goal is to keep the meeting brief.

2. **Set a reasonable time for everyone involved**. Make sure you choose the most opportune time for the family. Be flexible. This could mean Saturday morning or Sunday night at dinner. Some families choose to have Family Meeting after each dinner meal. Other families don't make a schedule; they have meetings whenever everyone is there. Adjust your meetings to fit your needs.

3. **Make Family Meeting fun**. There will be times that you will have to make a serious decision or discuss difficult issues. These should be infrequent, however. Concentrate on sharing information or praising the good things that other family members are doing.

4. **Use Preventive Teaching.** Teach your kids how to bring up topics for discussion before the meeting takes place. Practice what to say without offending or blaming someone else. Practice how to compliment others without sounding corny or insincere. And, teach your kids how to accept routine criticism without overreacting. This is a perfect time to teach your kids what to say and how to say it.

5. **Write it down**. Use some form of recordkeeping. Write decisions in a notebook, or find a convenient, well-visited spot to display them. Many parents choose to post schedules or announcements on the refrigerator door. Wonder what made them think anyone would see it there! Having a visible means of recordkeeping cuts down on confusion and keeps everyone informed.

6. **Give everyone a chance to speak**. You can teach cooperation, respect, and sensitivity by assuring everyone, from youngest to oldest, gets an equal voice in the way your family operates.

7. **Give positive consequences.** Give rewards and praise for listening to others, for not interrupting, for bringing up good suggestions, or for offering to help out. Family Meeting is an ideal time to praise your kids.

8. **Use all of your teaching skills during Family Meetings**. For example:

   • One of your kids receives minor criticism and begins to argue and make excuses—use Corrective Teaching.

   • If your child doesn't respond to Corrective Teaching, use Teaching Self-Control.

   • Review charts and contracts when following through on decisions.

   • Use Preventive Teaching before bringing up a sensitive issue or if your child has a problem giving opinions in front of others.

   • Use SODAS when solving problems.

Holding Family Meetings can be one of the most important times your family spends together. Your kids will feel more confident about sharing their opinions with others, about accepting compliments and criticism, and about making decisions. You will feel more organized and confident in your abilities, too. Start planning your first Family Meeting now, and you will be on the road to a happier, healthier family.

Notes

Chapter 15

Finishing Touches

Common Sense Parenting is practical and easy to use. Our research indicates that parents who complete our classes are more satisfied with their family life and report that their child's behavior has improved. Parents also find that they feel more positive about their children and more confident in their ability to deal with problems. This chapter contains tips for enhancing all of the skills learned in *Common Sense Parenting*. This information usually comes up during the parenting sessions and we feel it's valuable to be shared here.

Time with Your Children

Each of the skills outlined in Common Sense Parenting requires parents and children to spend time together. Time with your children may be the most important gift you can give them.

But, given the realities of family life today, finding time is not easy. For most families, jobs, activities and other commitments make it necessary for parents and their children to schedule time together if it is going to occur.

Try to set aside a special time each day for talking with your kids. And, more importantly, spend time listening to your kids. Let them talk openly and tell you how they feel about things. One way to accomplish this is to ask open-ended questions that prompt more than one-word answers. Then, listen attentively. This isn't a time for criticizing their decisions, but for asking them about their world—their ideas, their plans, and the important things in their lives. It's also a good time to share a little bit about your world, too.

Family Traditions

Family traditions are the core of what we remember about our families. These traditions and special events make each of our families unique. Going on family vacations, attending family reunions, going out to a favorite restaurant, and singing bedtime songs to the kids are all examples of special family traditions. The smell of the turkey at Thanksgiving, the Christmas traditions, summertime barbecues, visiting friends and relatives—these all make families special.

Here are a few of the traditions other families have shared with us:

- Going to midnight church services on Christmas Eve

- Eating popcorn and watching TV on Sunday evenings

- Honking the car horn whenever you drive through a tunnel

- Reading a story before going to bed

- Getting the special plate when you set the table for dinner

Exercise 1

Jot down a few of your family's traditions, or ones you would like to begin. Remember that they need not be holiday celebrations, just special times for you and your children.

1. _____

_____

2. _____

_____

3. _____

_____

4. _____

_____

5. _____

_____

One final note about traditions. Ask your kids to recall a favorite time with you. It's fun and interesting to hear what they have to say. Ask them to describe a family tradition or personal event that they find special. You may be amazed and amused at the memories they pick.

Consistency

Consistency is essential to successful parenting. Setting expectations, establishing and using consequences, and giving clear messages provides continuity and security in a child's life.

As parents, agree upon a common parenting approach. Often, parents disagree on how strict they should be, what rules to enforce, or what they should expect and accept from their kids. Parents will be more effective (and their kids will be less confused) when both parents have consistent expectations. If you feel like you need to clarify the rules you currently have, sit down with your spouse and start making a list you both agree on.

Perfection

There are no perfect parents. You're not. We're not. We're human beings and we're going to make mistakes, no matter how hard we try. The skills in *Common Sense Parenting* give us a plan for making fewer mistakes and doing better in the future.

Each parenting skill has steps to follow. Memorizing each step makes it easier to remember what to do. If you miss a step here or there, don't feel like you've failed. If you need to, go back and add the step you missed. The more you use these skills, the more comfortable you will become with them. Soon, each of the skills will be like second nature to you.

Parenting with Love

Trying to raise kids on love alone is not enough. Trying to raise kids using only the skills in this book is not enough, either. Together however, your love and *Common Sense Parenting* can be a powerful combination.

We can provide the information and the skills for you to use. But, only you can provide the most essential element—your love. And, all children need love, especially when it seems like they least deserve it.

It takes hard work to build a strong family. There are many heartaches and obstacles along the way. There also is much happiness and joy. Give yourself credit for all of the good things you do for your kids. Give yourself credit for trying to become a better parent. By combining your love with *Common Sense Parenting* skills, you can become the most influential teacher in your child's life.

Appendices

Positive Consequences That Cost No Money

Stay up late

Stay out late

Have a friend over

Go over to a friend's house

Extra TV (or video game) time

One less chore

Pick a movie

Mom or Dad read a story at night

Stay up late reading

Play game with Mom or Dad

Use car

Sleep in late

Extra phone time

Plan the menu

Special snacks

Sit at the head of the table

Messy room for a day

Leave radio on at night

Sleep downstairs or outside

Pick the TV program

Pick an outing

Shorter study period

Decide where to go for dinner

Trip to the library, zoo, pet store, park, etc.

Extra night out with friends

Permission for a special event

Dinner in the family room

Extra time on computer

Bike ride or fishing trip with parents

Indoor picnic

Pick the breakfast cereal

Go shopping (grocery)

Appendix B

Time-Out Guidelines for Parents

What is time-out?

Time-out is a way of disciplining your young child without raising your hand or your voice. Time-out involves removing your child from the good things in life, for a small amount of time, immediately after a misbehavior. Time-out for children is similar to penalties used for hockey players. When a hockey player has misbehaved on the ice, he is required to go to the penalty area for two minutes. The referee does not scream at, threaten, or hit the player. He merely blows the whistle and points to the penalty area. During the penalty time, the player is not allowed to play, only watch. Time-out bothers hockey players because they would rather play hockey than watch. Keep this hockey comparison in mind when using time-out for your child. Children usually don't like time-out because they would rather do things than watch other people doing things. So when you use time-out, remove your child from their immediate activity and seat them somewhere.

Where should the time-out area be?

You don't have to use the same place each time. Just make sure what you use is convenient for you. For example, using a downstairs chair is inconvenient when problem behavior occurs upstairs. An adult sized chair works best, but a step, footstool, bench, or couch will also work. Make sure the area is well lit and free from all dangerous objects. Also make sure your child cannot watch TV or play with toys (unless there is a political debate on and then, by all means, have them face your set).

How long should time-out last?

The upper limit should be one quiet minute for every year your child has been on planet earth. So if you have a two-year-old, aim for two quiet minutes. Keep in mind, children do not like time-out and they can be very public with their opinion. So it may take some time to get those two minutes. This is especially true in the beginning when children don't know the rules and still can't believe you are doing this to them. For some reason, the calmer you remain the more upset they are likely to become. This is all part of the process. Time-out works best when administered calmly.

So, do not begin the time until your child is calm and quiet. If your child is crying or throwing a tantrum, it doesn't count towards their required time. If you start the time because your child is quiet but your child starts to cry or throw a tantrum, wait until your child is quiet and start the time over again. Do not let them out of time-out until they have calmed down. Your child must remain seated and be quiet to get out of time-out. Some programs suggest using timers. Timers can be helpful but are not necessary. If you use one, remember the timer is to remind parents time-out is over, not children. You're the one who told your child to go to time-out; you tell your child when it's over.

What counts as quiet time?

Generally quiet time occurs when your child is not angry or mad. You must decide when your child is calm and quiet. Some children get perfectly still and quiet while in time-out. Other children find it hard to sit still and not talk. Fidgeting and "happy talk" should usually count as calm and quiet. If your son, for example, sings or talks softly to himself, that counts as quiet time.

What if your child leaves the chair before the time is up?

Say nothing. Calmly (and physically) return your child to the chair. In children between 2-4 years of age, unscheduled departures from the chair are a chronic early problem in the time-out process. Keep as calm as you can and keep returning them to the chair. If you tire or become angry, ask your spouse to assist you. If you are alone and become overly tired or angry, retreat with honor (for example, tell your child to stay down from the chair).

What if my child misbehaves in the chair?

Say nothing and ignore everyting that is not dangerous to child, self, and furniture. Most negative behavior in the chair is an attempt to get you to react and say something, anything. So expect the unexpected. Your child may whine, cry, complain, throw things, or make a big mess. They may make unkind comments about your parenting skills or say they don't love you any more. This last is perhaps the unkindest cut of all and, therefore, the hardest to ignore. Don't worry. They will love you again when their time is up.

When should I use time-out?

Use time-out as a consequence in the Corrective Teaching sequence. Immediately following a problem behavior, tell your child what he or she did and take (or in older children send) him or her to time-out. For example, you might say, "No hitting. Go to time-out." Say this calmly and only once. Do not reason or give long explanations to your child. If your child does not go willingly, take your child to time-out, using as little force as needed. For example, hold them gently by the hand or wrist and walk to the time-out area. Or, carry them facing away from you (so that there is no confusion between a hug and a trip to time-out). As suggested above, to avoid giving your child a lot of attention while being put in time-out, do not argue with, threaten, or spank your child.

What do I do when time is up?

When the time-out period is over, ask your child, "Are you ready to get up?" Your child must answer yes in some way (or nod yes) before you say that the child may get up. Go back and finish Corrective Teaching. Tell what you want him or her to do, and practice.

What do I do when my child is out of the chair?

The general rule for when time-out is over is to praise a good behavior. Now is the time to reward your child for the kinds of behaviors you want them to have. So catch 'em being good.

Should I explain the rules of time-out to my child?

Before using time-out, explain the rules to your child by using Preventive Teaching. At a time when your child is not misbehaving, explain what time-out is (simply), which problem behaviors time-out will be used for, and how long time-out will last. Practice using time-out with your child before using the procedure. While practicing, remind your child you are "pretending" this time. They will still go "ballistic" when do your first real time-outs but you'll be reassured that you've done your part to explain the fine print.

Summary

1. Choose time-out areas.

2. Explain time-out.

3. Use time-out *every* time the problem behaviors occur.

4. Be specific and brief when you explain why your child must go to time-out.

5. Do not talk to or look at your child during timeout.

6. If your child gets up from the chair, return him or her to the chair with no talking.

7. Your child must be calm and quiet to get up from time-out.

8. Your child must answer yes politely when you ask, "Would you like to get up?"

9. If you wanted your child to follow an instruction, give the child another chance after timeout is over.

10. Catch 'em being good.

Appendix C

Chores

Here is a list of chores that you can use as consequences that "add work." (See Chapter 5, "Negative Consequences.") Add work in areas that are different from the routine chores kids normally do as part of their family responsibilities.

Folding laundry

Putting laundry away

Making your brother's (sister's) bed

Vacuuming one (or several) rooms

Raking (all or part of) the yard

Mowing the grass

Taking out the trash

Collecting the trash from throughout the house

Helping your brother (sister) with his chores

Dusting furniture

Sweeping the porch

Washing (some or all) the windows

Washing the car

Vacuuming the carpet in the car

Washing the car windows

Cleaning the garage

Helping your brother (sister) put toys away

Emptying the dishwasher

Loading the dishwasher

Sweeping the kitchen (dining room) floor

Cleaning the bathroom sink, tub, shower, toilet, and/or floor

Cleaning the kitchen sink

Cleaning the bedroom

Shaking the rugs

These consequences can vary in amount or degree. Take into account the age and ability of your kids. Also, adjust the consequence to fit the severity of the problem behavior. Remember to use the smallest consequence necessary to change the behavior.

One variation that parents tell us works well is the "chore jar." Many parents use the chore jar for their child's common misbehaviors like talking back or not following directions right away. Parents write various chores on small pieces of paper and put them in the jar. When their child misbehaves, the parents use Corrective Teaching. But, when they reach the consequence portion of Corrective Teaching, the child picks a chore from the jar. This makes it easier for parents since the consequences are made up and readily available. It works best if parents tell their kids ahead of time about the chore jar and how it will work.

Some parents use a second jar to place the slips of paper after a chore has been completed. Then, when all of the slips of paper are emptied from the first jar, another chore jar is ready to use.

One way to use the list as a positive consequence is to schedule a "No Chores" day to reward some or all of your children for doing well.

Skills for Children and Teens

1. Following Instructions
2. Accepting Criticism
3. Accepting "No" Answers
4. Staying Calm
5. Disagreeing with Others
6. Asking for Help
7. Asking Permission
8. Getting Along with Others
9. Apologizing
10. Conversation Skills
11. Giving Compliments
12. Accepting Compliments
13. Listening to Others
14. Telling the Truth
15. Introducing Yourself

Following Instructions

When you are given an instruction, you should:

1. **Look at the person who is talking.**

2. **Show that you understand** ("I understand," "OK," or "I'll do it"). Make sure you wait until the person is done talking before you do what is asked. It is usually best to answer, but sometimes nodding your head will be enough to show the person that you understand.

3. **Do what is asked in the best way that you can.**

4. **Let the person know that you have finished.**

It is important to do what is asked because it shows your ability to cooperate and it saves time. Following instructions will help you in school, in the home, with adults and with friends.

Helpful Hints:

• After finding out exactly what has been asked, start the task immediately.

• If you have any doubts that doing what is asked will result in some type of negative consequence for you or you don't understand, ask a trusted adult.

• Do what is asked as pleasantly as possible.

• Check back as soon as you finish. This increases the chances that you will get credit for doing a job well. It also means that somebody else doesn't have time to mess it up before you check back.

Accepting Criticism

When others tell you how they think you can improve, they give you criticism. When you accept criticism, you should:

1. **Look at the person.** Don't give negative facial expressions.

2. **Remain calm and quiet while the person is talking.**

3. **Show that you understand.** ("OK", or "I understand.")

4. **Try to correct the problem.** If you are asked to do something different, do it. If you are asked to stop doing something, stop it. If you can't give a positive response; at least give one that will not get you into trouble ("OK," "I understand," or "Thanks").

Being able to accept criticism shows maturity and prevents having problems with people in authority. If you can control yourself and listen to what others have to say about how you can improve, it will result in fewer problems for you. And, the criticism may really help you!

Helpful Hints:

- It is most important that you stay calm. Take a deep breath if necessary.

- Giving criticism back, becoming angry, or making negative facial expressions will only get you into more trouble.

- When you respond to the person who is giving you criticism, use a pleasant voice tone as much as possible. You will receive criticism for the rest of your life—all people do. The way you handle it determines how you are treated by others.

- Most criticism is designed to help you; however, sometimes it is hard to accept. If you don't agree with the criticism, ask me or another trusted adult.

- Always ask questions if you don't understand (but don't play games by asking questions when you really do understand it and are just being stubborn.) Give yourself a chance to improve!

Accepting 'No' Answers

1. **Look at the person.**

2. **Say "OK."**

3. **Calmly ask for a reason if you really don't understand.**

4. **If you disagree, bring it up later.**

You will be told "No" many times in your life. Getting angry and upset only leads to more problems. If you are able to appropriately accept the "No" answer, people will view you as cooperative and mature.

Helpful Hints:

- Don't stare, make faces or look away. If you are upset, control your emotions. Try to relax and stay calm. Listening carefully will help you understand what the other person is saying.

- Answer right away and speak clearly. Take a deep breath if you feel upset.

- Don't ask for a reason every time or you will be viewed as a complainer. People will think you are serious about wanting to know a reason if you ask for one calmly. Don't keep asking for reasons after you receive one. Use what you learn in these situations in the future.

- Take some time to plan how you are going to approach the person who told you "No." Plan in advance what you are going to say. Accept the answer, even if it is still "No." Be sure to thank the person for listening. At least you had the opportunity to share your opinion.

Staying Calm

When people feel angry or upset, it's hard to stay calm. When we feel like "blowing up," we sometimes make poor choices. And, usually, when we make poor choices, we regret it later. If you feel that you are going to lose self-control, you should:

1. **Take a deep breath.**

2. **Relax your muscles.**

3. **Tell yourself to "Be calm," or count to ten.**

4. **Share your feelings.** After you are relaxed, tell someone you trust what is bothering you.

5. **Try to solve the situation that made you upset.**

It is important to stay calm since worse things always seem to happen if you lose your temper. If you can stay calm, other people will depend on you more often. They will see you as mature and able to handle even the worst situations. Teachers and employers will respect you and look upon you as someone who can keep "cool."

Helpful Hints:

- You might try to talk yourself into the idea that "blowing up" is the only thing to do. The other person or thing "deserves it." Forget it. It doesn't work that way. And, you're setting yourself up to get more or worse consequences. Be calm.

- After you have calmed down, pat yourself on the back. Even adults have a hard time with self-control. If you can control yourself, you will have accomplished something that many adults are still struggling with. Give yourself some praise! You have done the right thing.

Disagreeing with Others

When you don't agree with another person's opinion or decision, you should:

1. **Remain calm.** Getting upset will only make matters worse.

2. **Look at the person.** This shows that you have confidence.

3. **Begin with a positive or neutral statement.** "I know you are trying to be fair but..."

4. **Explain why you have a disagreement with the decision.** Keep your voice tone level and controlled. Be brief and clear.

5. **Listen as the other person explains his or her side of the story.**

6. **Calmly accept whatever decision is made.**

7. **Thank the person for listening, regardless of the outcome.**

It is important to disagree in a calm manner because it increases the chances that the other person will listen. This may be the only opportunity you have to get the decision changed. You have a right to be able to express your opinions. But, you lose that right if you become upset or aggressive. If the other person feels that you are going to become out of control, you stand very little chance of getting your views across.

Helpful Hints:

- You're not going to win every time. Some decisions will not change. However, learning how to disagree calmly may help change some of them.

- Don't try to change everything. People will view you as a pest.

- If you are calm and specific when you disagree, people will respect you for the mature way you handle situations. It pays off in the long run!

Asking for Help

When you need help with something, you should:

1. **Decide what the problem is.**

2. **Ask to speak to the person most likely to help you.**

3. **Look at the person, clearly describe what you need help with, and ask the person in a pleasant voice tone.**

4. **Thank the person for helping you.**

It is important to ask help from others because it is the best way to solve problems you can't figure out. Asking for help in a pleasant manner means you are more likely to have someone help you.

Helpful Hints:

- It is nice to figure things out by yourself. Sometimes, this isn't possible. Asking someone who has more experience, or has had more success with a similar problem, is a way to learn how to solve the problem the next time.

- Sometimes, people become frustrated when they can't figure something out. Sometimes, they even become mad. Learn to ask for help before you get to this point and you will have more successes than failures.

- Always tell the person who is helping you how much you appreciate the help. It might be nice to offer your help the next time that person needs something.

Asking Permission

When you need to get permission from someone else, you should:

1. Look at the other person.

2. **Be specific when you ask permission**. The other person should know exactly what you are requesting.

3. **Be sure to ask rather than demand.** "May I please...?"

4. **Give reasons if necessary.**

5. **Accept the decision.**

It is important to ask permission whenever you want to do something or use something that another person is responsible for. Asking permission shows your respect for another person and increases the chances that your request will be granted.

Helpful Hints:

• If you don't own something, it always is wise to ask permission to use it. It doesn't matter if it is a sack of potato chips or someone's bike, ask permission!

• Sometimes you won't get what you want, but if you have asked permission politely and correctly, it is more likely that you may get what you want the next time.

• It may help you to remember how you would feel if someone used something of yours without asking first. Other than feeling like that person was not polite or respectful of your property, something could get broken or lost.

Getting Along with Others

To be successful in dealing with people, you should:

1. **Listen to what the other person says.**

2. **Say something positive if you agree with what that person said. If you don't agree, say something that won't end up in an argument.** Use a calm voice tone.

3. **Show interest in what the other person has to say.** Try to understand his or her point of view.

It is important to get along with others because you will be working and dealing with other people for most of your life. If you can get along with others, it is more likely that you will be successful in whatever you do. Getting along with others shows sensitivity and respect. If you can get along with others, it is more likely that they will behave the same way. In other words, treat others the way you want to be treated!

Helpful Hints:

• Sometimes it is not easy to get along with others. If someone does something that you do not like, or says something negative, you may feel like behaving the same way. Don't! Stop yourself from saying things that can hurt others' feelings. Teasing, cussing, and insults will only make matters worse. It is better to ignore others' negative behavior than to act like them.

• Getting along with others takes some effort. It is hard to understand why some people act the way they do. Try to put yourself in their place and maybe it will be easier to understand.

• If you find that you don't like someone's behavior, it is better to say nothing than something negative.

Apologizing

When you have done something that hurts another person's feelings or that results in negative consequences for another person, you should apologize.

1. Look at the person. It shows confidence.

2. Say what you are sorry about. "I'm sorry I said that" or "I'm sorry, I didn't listen to what you said."

3. Make a follow-up statement if the person says something to you. "Is there any way I can make it up to you?" or "It won't happen again."

4. Thank the person for listening. (Even if the person did not accept your apology!)

It is important to apologize because it shows that you are sensitive to other's feelings. It increases the chances that other people will be sensitive to your feelings in return. Apologizing also shows that you are responsible enough to admit to making a mistake.

Helpful Hints:

• It is easy to avoid making apologies; it takes guts to be mature enough to do it. Convince yourself that making an apology is the best thing to do and then do it!

• If the other person is upset with you, the response you receive may not be real nice at that time. Be prepared to take whatever the other person says. Be confident that you are doing the right thing.

• When people look back on your apology, they will think that you were able to realize what you had done wrong. They will think more positively of you in the future.

• An apology won't erase what you did wrong to begin with. But, it may help change a person's opinion of you in the long run.

Conversation Skills

When you are talking with other people, you should:

1. **Look at the other person.**

2. **Answer any questions asked of you, and give complete answers.** Just saying "yes" or "no," does not give the other person any information that can keep the conversation going.

3. **Avoid negative statements.** Talking about past trouble you were in, bragging, name calling, cussing, or making other negative statements gives a bad impression.

4. **Use appropriate grammar.** Slang can be used with friends, but don't use it when guests are present.

5. **Start or add to conversation by asking questions, talking about new or exciting events, or asking the other person what he or she thinks about something.**

It is important to have good conversation skills because you can tell others what you think about something and get their feelings about something. Good conversation skills make guests feel more comfortable and visits with you more enjoyable. Conversation skills also help you when you apply for a job or meet new people.

Helpful Hints:

- Always include the other person's ideas in the conversation. If you don't, it won't be a conversation!

- Smile and show interest in what the other person has to say, even if you don't agree with the person.

- Keep up on current events so that you have a wide range of things to talk about. People who can talk about what's happening and are good at conversation are usually well-liked and admired by other people.

Giving Compliments

When you say something nice about other people, you should:

1. **Look at the other person.**

2. **Give the compliment.** Tell him or her exactly what you liked.

3. **Make a follow-up statement.** If the person says "Thanks," say "You're welcome," in return.

Giving compliments to others shows that you can notice the accomplishments of someone else. It shows friendliness; people like being around someone who is pleasant and can say nice things. It also shows that you have confidence in your ability to talk to others.

Helpful Hints:

- Think of the exact words you want to use before you give the compliment. It will make you feel more confident and less likely to fumble around for words.

- Mean what you say. People can tell the difference between real and phony.

- Don't overdo it. A couple of sentences will do. "You did a good job at..." or "You really did well in..."

- It is nice to smile and be enthusiastic when you give compliments. It makes the other person feel that you really mean it.

Accepting Compliments

Whenever someone says something nice to you, you should:

1. **Look at the other person.**

2. **Listen to what the other person is saying.**

3. **Don't interrupt.**

4. **Say "Thanks," or something that shows you appreciate what was said.**

Being able to accept compliments shows that you can politely receive another person's opinion about something you have done. It also increases the chance that you will receive future compliments.

Helpful Hints:

• Many times it is easy to feel uncomfortable when you receive a compliment. For example, when someone gives you a compliment on a sweater you are wearing, and you say, "Whattya mean, this old rag?" Statements like that make the other person less likely to give you compliments in the future. Don't reject what the other person is saying.

• People give compliments for a variety of reasons. Don't waste a lot of time wondering why someone gave you a compliment. Just appreciate the fact that someone took the time to say something nice to you!

Listening to Others

When others are speaking, you should:

1. **Look at the person who is talking.**

2. **Sit or stand quietly.**

3. **Wait until the person is through talking.** Don't interrupt, it will seem like you are complaining.

4. **Show that you understand.** ("OK," "Thanks," "I see," etc.) or ask the person to explain if you don't understand.

It is important to listen because it shows pleasantness and cooperation. It increases the chances that people will listen to you. And, it increases the chances that you will do the correct thing since you understand.

Helpful Hints:

- If you are having trouble listening, think of how you would feel if other people didn't listen to you.

- Try to remember everything the person said. Write it down if you feel you may forget.

- People who learn to listen well do better on jobs and in school.

- Don't show any negative facial expressions. Continue looking at the other person, and nod your head or occasionally say something to let the other person know you are still listening.

Telling the Truth

When you have done something, whether it's good or bad, you need to tell the truth. Telling the truth makes other people trust you. If they can believe what you say, you will be able to be trusted in more situations. Sometimes, people will ask you questions about your involvement in a situation. To tell the truth you should:

1. **Look at the person.**

2. **Say exactly what happened if asked to supply information.**

3. **Answer any other questions.** This can be what you did or did not do, or what someone else did or did not do.

4. **Don't leave out important facts.**

5. **Admit to mistakes or errors if you made them.**

It is important to tell the truth because people are more likely to give you a second chance if they have been able to trust you in the past. We all make mistakes—but trying to avoid telling the truth will lead to more problems. If you get the reputation of a liar, it is hard for people to believe what you say. Plus, when you tell the truth, you should feel confident that you have done the right thing.

Helpful Hints:

- Telling the truth is hard. Many times, it will seem that lying is the easiest way out of a situation. When people find out that you have lied, the consequences are much worse.

- Lying is the opposite of telling the truth. Lying is similar to stealing or cheating. All will result in negative consequences for you.

Introducing Yourself

When you introduce yourself to others, you should:

1. **Stand up straight.** If you were sitting down or doing something else, stop immediately and greet the person.

2. **Look at the other person.**

3. **Offer your hand and shake hands firmly.** (Don't wait!)

4. **Say your name as you are shaking hands, clearly and loudly enough to be heard easily.** This shows the other person that you are confident.

5. **Make a friendly statement.** ("Nice to meet you.")

It is important to introduce yourself because it shows your ability to meet new people confidently. It makes others feel more comfortable and you make a good first impression. Being able to introduce yourself will be helpful on job interviews and is a pleasant way to "break the ice."

Helpful Hints:

- Being pleasant is very important when introducing yourself. If you are gruff or your voice is harsh, people won't get a good impression of you. Smile when giving your name to the other person.

- Introductions are the first step in conversation. If you start out on the right foot, it is more likely that you will have a pleasant conversation. Make your first impression a good impression.

- If the other person does not give his or her name, say "And your name is?"

- After you have met a person once, you will have to choose how to re-introduce yourself. If there is a long time in between, or if the person may have forgotten, then you should follow the same steps as above. If the time in between is short, you may choose just to say, "Hi, in case you forgot, I'm _____ ."

- Try to remember the other person's name. Other people will be impressed when you take enough time to remember them.